Soccer School

Name: ....

Class: ....

Coaches: ....

Kickito Ergo Sum

To Oisín, Rohan, and Aoife
A. B.
To Sonny, Ollo, and G.G.
B. L.
For Kaz, Ethan, and Stevie
S. G.

Text copyright © 2017 by Alex Bellos and Ben Lyttleton
Illustrations copyright © 2017 by Spike Gerrell

First U.S. paperback edition 2019

Library of Congress Catalog Card Number 2018960064
ISBN 978-1-5362-0436-0 (hardcover)
ISBN 978-1-5362-0875-7 (paperback)

19 20 21 22 23 24 MNG 10 9 8 7 6 5 4 3 2 1

Printed in Saline, MI, U.S.A.

This book was typeset in Palatino.
The illustrations were done in ink with digital manipulation.

Walker Books U.S.
a division of
Candlewick Press
99 Dover Street
Somerville, Massachusetts 02144

www.walkerbooksus.com

S⚽CCER SCHOOL

season 2

WHERE SOCCER ~~EXPLAINS~~ Saves THE WORLD

Alex Bellos & Ben Lyttleton

illustrated by Spike Gerrell

WALKER BOOKS

You're going to be amazed by:

the women who were once the most famous soccer players in Great Britain . . .

and the most awesome stadiums in the world.

In order to find the best soccer stories, we have spoken to lots of brilliant people.

Like the player who speaks EIGHT languages.

And the best mower in the English Premier League.

You will also meet our star students. They are outstanding in their subjects!

We have a quiz at the end of each lesson. You can be a star student too if you get the answers right. We bet you'll get more right than your friends and family.

Extra! Extra! This season we have introduced after-school clubs, with lots of activities you can do at home.

They will exercise your muscles and your mind.

Because everything at Soccer School is designed to make you a better player.

And a smarter one too!

MEET YOUR COACHES

ALEX "BELLINHOS" BELLOS

66 Tudo bem, amigo? 99

☆☆☆ coach stats

Birthplace: Oxford, England

Height: 5 ft. 8 in. / 173 cm

Color of hair: Black

Favorite number: 22

Cool fact about home: Can see Wembley Stadium from his window

Favorite school subject: Math

Favorite book while in school: The Hobbit

Ball-juggling record: 22

Favorite player: Garrincha (Brazil)

Favorite player's haircut: Marouane Fellaini (curly and proud of it!)

Favorite goal: Archie Gemmill for Scotland against the Netherlands in the 1978 World Cup

Soccer dream: For Heart of Midlothian to win the Champions League

coach stats

Birthplace: London

Height: 6 ft. / 183 cm

Color of hair: Brown

Favorite number: 8

Cool fact about home: There's a park at the end of his road for extra soccer practice.

Favorite school subject: English

Favorite book while in school: Treasure Island

Ball-juggling record: 94

Favorite player: Ousmane Dembélé (France)

Favorite player's haircut: The mullet (short sides, long at back) worn by the 1990s England player Chris Waddle

Favorite goal: Antonin Panenka's chipped penalty in the 1976 European Championships

Soccer dream: Getting the call-up to play for England

BEN "THE PEN" LYTTLETON

"Penalty, ref!"

CLASS SCHEDULE

	MONDAY	TUESDAY
HOMEROOM		
1st PERIOD	**HEALTH** 1	**HISTORY** 44
2nd PERIOD		
3rd PERIOD	**FOREIGN LANGUAGES** 12	**BOTANY** 56
4th PERIOD		
LUNCH		
5th PERIOD	**PHYSICS** 30	**FILM STUDIES** 68
AFTER-SCHOOL CLUBS	**FEET** 42	**MIND** 82

Are you as smart as our star students?

WEDNESDAY	THURSDAY	FRIDAY
8:30–8:40 AM		
ENGINEERING 84	BIOLOGY 128	ART 168
ENGLISH 100	MATH 142	
1:00–2:00 PM		
RELIGIOUS STUDIES 112	PSYCHOLOGY 154	BUSINESS STUDIES 180
BALANCE 126	HEALTH 166	RECOVERY 192

Find the answers to the quizzes on page 196. But no cheating!

Hello, everyone! It's the beginning of Season 2 at Soccer School, and we're going to start by revealing a stinky ritual that soccer players perform at the beginning of every season.

Professional soccer players must provide their teams with small tubes of their finest pee!

Can you imagine it? Yuck!

But it's true. The players all head to the bathroom, where each of them piddles into a small container. They hand over the flask of their warm, golden liquid to the team doctors, who test it.

Pee is mostly water, but it also contains small amounts of other substances. Doctors check these substances for health problems such as infections, diabetes, and diseases, which may otherwise go unnoticed.

In this lesson, we'll find out what you can learn from your pee. We'll be looking at the water system in our bodies: fluids go in, fluids go out, and fluids go all about.

Are you thirsty for this knowledge? Drink up!

WATER WORKS

Water has no color, no taste, and no smell. Sounds like a really boring liquid!

But that's not true. Water keeps us alive. Inside our bodies, water is working nonstop doing all these jobs:

- Making our food mushy so it can pass through our digestive system
- Helping blood and nutrients circulate around our body
- Regulating our body temperature
- Making our joints move smoothly
- Removing waste products in pee

Water does so much for us that we need lots of it. In fact, water makes up about 60 percent of our body weight. Humans aren't all flesh and blood. We're mostly water!

A healthy adult can go without food for about a month, provided they are allowed water. (We don't recommend trying it!) But an adult can go without water for only a little more than a week. Humans need water to survive.

A SWEATY JOB

Water goes into our bodies in the form of food and drink.

Water leaves our bodies in our pee and sweat. There are also small amounts in our poop and breath. We'll come to pee later, but first, here's the juice about sweat.

Sweat is the body's tool for cooling itself down. When the weather is hot or we're exercising, our bodies warm up and we sweat.

Sweat is made up almost entirely of water, with a pinch of salt, which is why it tastes a bit salty. On the surface of our skin are millions of **sweat glands**, which are tiny tubes that produce sweat. When sweat comes out of the glands, it appears on the outside of the skin. Once the sweat is on the skin's surface, it starts to disappear into the air through a process called **evaporation**. When the sweat evaporates, it takes the heat from your body. And when the body loses heat, it cools down.

The hotter our bodies get, the more we sweat. Everyone sweats different amounts. It depends on things like your build and fitness levels.

Athletes sweat a lot. Soccer players sweat one to two quarts/liters during a game, which is equivalent to four to eight glasses of water. In the summer, players can sweat up to four quarts/liters, or sixteen glasses of water, which is around 5 percent of their body weight in sweat. Phew!

WATER LEVELS

If we have the right amount of water in our bodies, we say we are **hydrated**. If we have too little water in our bodies from sweating or not drinking enough, we are **dehydrated**.

It is never good to be dehydrated. It can give you headaches, increase tiredness, make you lose concentration, and PUT YOU IN A REALLY BAD MOOD. You don't want to see Alex when he's dehydrated!

Soccer players are careful to avoid dehydration because it affects their game. One team doctor told us that a 5 percent reduction in the amount of water in a body can result in a 20 percent drop in performance. On the field, dehydration can cause:

⚽ Slower reaction times

⚽ Poor coordination

⚽ Reduced control of the joints

⚽ Increased chance of strains and sprains

For players to stay properly hydrated, they need to make sure they replace the water lost through sweating. That's why players are often sipping drinks during stops in play.

TAKING THE PEE

The other main way our bodies lose water is through the **urinary system**, which makes pee.

The important organs in the urinary system are the **kidneys** and the **bladder**. We are born with two kidneys, although we only need one to be working in order to have a normal life. **Urine**, or pee, is made in the kidneys, and then travels to the bladder via the **ureter**. When the bladder is nearly full, our brain tells us we need to go to the bathroom. Pee passes out of the body through the **urethra**.

Hurry up!

TO PEE OR NOT TO PEE?

Urine can show signs of disease and infection, which is why team doctors check their players' pee. Urine can also contain evidence that players have been taking **performance-enhancing drugs**, which are banned.

If someone is taking drugs, those drugs get in the person s bloodstream. The kidneys will extract them and put them in the person s pee. There's no hiding when it comes to the urinary system.

For this reason, professional players are often asked to provide a urine sample during practice or right after a game. The pee police—known as **Doping Control Officers (DCO)**—then check the sample for any banned chemicals.

When a DCO asks a player for a urine sample, the officer must watch the player peeing into the tube, so they know it is fresh pee and not pee they could have stored earlier or gotten from someone else.

But some people find it very difficult to pee when they are being watched! Players also have to pee a certain amount, so if they have sweated a lot, they will need to drink lots in order to produce their sample, which can result in the player vomiting or peeing all night. One team doctor told us that sometimes players have taken hours to pee, which causes them huge embarrassment, since it can hold up the whole team from going home.

THANKS, DAD

Our kidneys are essential to our survival—so it's a good thing we have two. If one kidney stops working, you can get by with just the other one. But if both stop working, then you will need to have a **kidney transplant**, which is when a healthy kidney is taken from someone else and put into your body. Sometimes a person's body will accept the new kidney, and that person may be able to regain full health. But sometimes the body will reject it, in which case another transplant is needed.

In 2007, Croatian striker Ivan Klasnić was diagnosed with kidney failure. His mom decided to give him one of her kidneys, but Ivan's body rejected it. Then his father gave him one of his and it worked. Klasnić recovered well enough to play for Croatia at the Euro 2008 tournament and scored two goals in the competition, making him the first kidney transplant patient to compete at a major tournament. Sadly, however, his father's kidney stopped working properly in 2016, and Klasnić had to have a third transplant.

URINE GOAL

Argentine goalkeeper Sergio Goycochea had a wee-ird habit before penalty shoot-outs. He would crouch behind the line in his own goal and pee onto the field through his shorts. The first time he did it was in the 1990 World Cup quarterfinal against Yugoslavia, and he saved two penalties and one hit the crossbar.

A few days later, he did the same trick in the semifinal against competition host Italy, and he saved two more. "It was my lucky charm," he said.

WILLIE P. STAINES

☆ STAR ☆ STUDENT

66 Fancy a drink? 99

☆☆☆ STAR STUDENT **Stats**

Longest pee: 1 min. 52 sec.
Bladder capacity: 1 pint/500 ml
Number of sweat glands: 2 million
Daily water intake: 6 cups/1.5 l
Birthplace: Pee Pee Creek, Ohio
Supports: Waterford FC (Ireland)
Fave player: Boy Waterman
Trick: Dribbles everywhere

HEALTH QUIZ

1. What is the scientific name for pee?

a) Bile
b) Feces
c) Mucus
d) Urine

2. Which part of the body has no sweat glands?

a) The nose
b) The lips
c) The ears
d) The palms
   of the hands

3. The chemical formula for water is H_2O. What do the H and the O stand for?

a) Hydrogen and Oxygen
b) Hippo and Octopus
c) Humid and Omnipresent
d) Hazard and Özil

4. Which food gives your pee a strong smell?

a) Asparagus
b) Eggplant
c) Avocado
d) Beets

5. Which of these is correct?

a) Peeing was a competitive sport in ancient Greece.
b) The ancient Romans used pee to whiten their teeth.
c) The ancient Egyptians used pee as a perfume.
d) Pee soup is an ancient British delicacy.

FOREIGN LANGUAGES

Everyone speaks soccer.

If you go on vacation to another country, it is possible to have a game against the locals even if no one understands a word anyone else is saying.

In fact, it is possible to be on the same soccer team as someone and not understand a word they are saying. And this happens quite a lot now in professional soccer. Top teams have players from many different countries who speak many different languages. Sometimes two players may not have a language in common. So if they are together — next to each other at dinner, on the bench, or on the team bus — they may not be able to communicate with words at all. When coaches are unable to speak the same language as the players, they use an interpreter to translate what they are saying in order for their players to understand them. (Eventually players will pick up words of the local language, but learning new words takes time.)

In this lesson, we're going to look at why there are so many different languages and how they are created. You'll also learn about chickens in Brazil.

Let's go! *Los geht's! ¡Vamos! Allons-y!*

SPREAD THE WORD

Most scientists think modern humans originated in Africa within the last two hundred thousand years. These early groups of people did lots of exploring. It is believed that they and their descendants gradually walked out of Africa and settled all over the world.

Our earliest ancestors probably grunted and squeaked at one another. From these funny noises emerged spoken language, which is a system of words like the ones we use now. One theory is that the first humans to speak all used the same language, but as they moved from Africa around the world, this early language evolved into other languages, which then changed into even more languages. Language is always changing as speakers replace old words with new words. If you add too many new words to a language, it becomes a different one! The world now has about seven thousand spoken languages.

You can see how much languages change by looking at English over the last few hundred years. Here are some of language expert Mark Forsyth's favorite words that we don't use anymore. We love them too — Alex fudgels all the time!

OLD WORD	WHEN AND WHERE	MEANING
Fudgel	1700s, England	To pretend to work when you're not
Gongoozle	1940s, England	To stare lazily at a canal and do nothing
Groke	1800s, Scotland	To look at someone who's eating in the hope they will give you some food
Snollygoster	1800s, United States	A dishonest politician
Wamblecropt	1500s, England	Overcome with indigestion

And lots of new words—which your great-great-great grandparents would never have heard—have now entered the language:

NEW WORD	MEANING
Clickbait	A website link that's designed to attract attention and encourage people to read on
Emoji	A small image used to express an emotion or idea in electronic communication
Olinguito	A raccoon-like animal from South America that was discovered in 2013
Squee	A high-pitched squealing sound
YOLO	Short for "You only live once," an expression that means you should have fun now and not think about the future

Emoji

Olinguito

Squee

SOUNDS THE SAME

In Europe there are about forty main languages. Many are quite similar to one another. For example, French, Spanish, Portuguese, Italian, and Romanian have many words in common because they are all descended from Latin, the language of the ancient Romans. English and German have many similarities, as do Swedish, Norwegian, Danish, and Icelandic.

Often countries that are close to each other geographically have similar words for the same thing. This is because people living near one another share and borrow words, just as they might trade goods. For example, consider the word *football*, which most of the world uses to mean soccer. It was first used in English about five hundred years ago.

THE WORLD OF
FOOTBALL

SOCCER
(USA)

FUTEBOL
(Portugal)

The game of football—or soccer—didn't exist at that time, so *football*

referred to a "round object to play with" using one's foot.

But by the late nineteenth century, *football* meant the game of soccer we know and love today. As the game became popular around the world, many different countries started talking about it and introduced the word *football* into their languages. But they changed the word a little bit, so it would fit with their local rules for spelling and pronunciation.

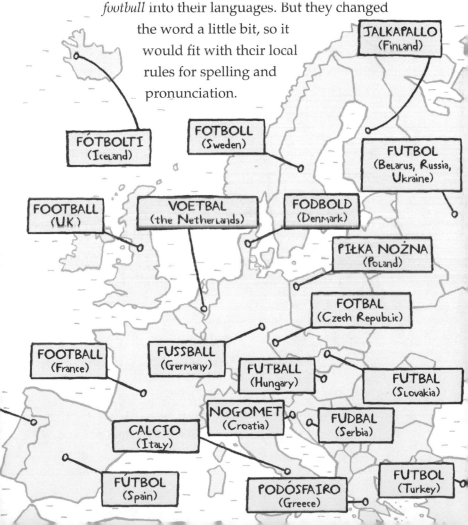

THE ODDBALLS

As you can see from the map on the previous page, some countries have their own words for football that look nothing like *football*. Here are some of the reasons why:

Soccer (United States): In the mid-1800s, Rugby School, in England, invented a twist on English football: Rugby football, which used an oval ball and allowed handling. Regular football was organized by the Football Association, so to differentiate the old game from the newfangled Rugby version, it came to be known as Association football. And then the word *soccer* was coined from the word *Association*. For a long time in the U.K., the words *football* and *soccer* were used interchangeably, but *soccer* became less and less common. In the United States, though, we say *soccer,* since *football* refers to a quite different American game. Got it?

Calcio **(Italy):** *Calcio fiorentino* was a violent ball game with twenty-seven players per team that originated in the Italian city of Florence in the sixteenth century. Brits founded Genoa, the first Italian soccer team, in 1893, but Italian officials didn't want to use the foreign word *football* to name the sport. So they stuck with *calcio*, from the Italian word *calciare*, meaning to kick. *Calcio fiorentino*, now called *calcio storico* ("historic football"), is still played in the summer in Florence.

Nogomet (**Croatia**): A combination of the Croatian words *noga* (meaning foot) and *meta* (meaning target). It was coined in the late 1890s by linguist Slavko Rutzner-Radmilović, who was eating cake in a Zagreb bakery when out of the window he saw some students kicking a ball around in a park. The term was used interchangeably with *footbull* for a while, but the first soccer team in Zagreb, PNIŠK, was founded with *nogomet* (and not *football*) in its name. All other teams in Croatia then adopted *nogomet* in their names too.

Piłka nożna (**Poland**): The Polish name for soccer literally means "ball leggy." *Piłka* means ball and *nożna* is a descriptive word, or adjective, which comes from *noga*, meaning leg. It was an incorrect translation of the word *football*, but became widely used after the first Polish radio broadcast of a soccer game in 1929.

TONGUE TWISTERS

Professional soccer has become such an international game that players now often move from one country to another several times in their careers. Sometimes teams provide **interpreters** to help players who do not speak the local language. But often players learn to speak the lingo. The ones in the table on the opposite page really have the gift of gab!

The top linguist of his soccer generation is Croatian midfielder Ivan Rakitić, who has won the top European tournaments La Liga and the Champions League with his team Barcelona and speaks EIGHT languages! We interviewed him to find out how he became multi-multi-lingual!

IVAN, THE TERRIBLY GOOD AT LANGUAGES

How do you know so many languages, Ivan?

My parents spoke Croatian, and I grew up in Switzerland, where many languages are spoken. Now my wife is Spanish and we speak Spanish at home! Communication is important on a team, and I've always wanted to learn the language of the team where I am playing, as well as teammates' home languages.

What is your favorite word?

Love / amor / ljubav / Liebe / amour / amore

PLAYER	NUMBER OF LANGUAGES	LANGUAGES
Nadia Nadim (Denmark)	9	Arabic, Danish, Dari, English, French, German, Hindi, Persian, Urdu
Ivan Rakitić (Croatia)	8	Catalan, Croatian, English, French, German, Italian, Spanish, Swiss-German
Gelson Fernandes (Switzerland)	8	Cape Verde Creole, English, French, German, Italian, Portuguese, Spanish, Swiss-German
Mikel Arteta (Spain)	7	Basque, Catalan, English, French, Italian, Portuguese, Spanish
Philippe Senderos (Switzerland)	7	English, French, German, Italian, Serbian, Spanish, Swiss-German

What language do you dream in?

A mix of all of them!

Do your teammates call you "the Dictionary"?

No, but it is great to be able to speak to people in their mother tongue, especially when they have just arrived on a team. It helps them settle in and feel at home more quickly.

Will you work as an interpreter when you retire?

I still have a lot of soccer to play, so am focused on my playing career, but I hope to work in a job with an international profile requiring several languages and travel once I stop playing.

TV

SOCCER SCHOOL

WONDERFUL WORLD OF WORDS

Languages need to have words for basic, everyday things such as hand, table, and sun. But sometimes you get amazing words that only exist in one language. Here are some of our favorites—we wish English had them!

WORD	LANGUAGE	REGION	MEANING
Abanyawoih-warrgahmarnegan-jginjeng	Bininj Gun-wok	Northern Australia	I cooked the wrong meat for them again
Embasan	Maguindanao	Philippines	To take a bath with your clothes on
Hanyauku	Rukwangali	Namibia	To walk on warm sand on your tiptoes
Ribuytibuy	Mundari	India and Bangladesh	The sound, sight, or motion of a big person's buttocks rubbing together as they walk
Zhaghzhagh	Persian	Iran	The chattering of teeth from the cold or from anger

WOBBLE

RUB

Aaargh! My eyes!

WORDS OF HOPE

Here's a tip for players who find learning a second language difficult. Learn Esperanto! It is a language that was invented to be as simple as possible to learn.

Polish doctor Ludwik Zamenhof created Esperanto in 1887. He wanted to make it easier for people of different nationalities to communicate, as he thought it would make everyone nicer to each other. The language came to be called Esperanto—which is Esperanto for "one who hopes."

Many hundreds of thousands of people can speak the language—at least a little bit. And Esperanto even has its own soccer team, made up of speakers from Argentina, Brazil, the Czech Republic, France, Hungary, Nepal, Slovakia, Switzerland, and Taiwan.

When it comes to soccer, different languages often use different phrases to describe what goes on in the game. Turn the page for our favorite entries from the *ABCD (IE)*, which is short for *Alex and Ben's Classroom Dictionary (International Edition)*.

Alex and Ben's Classroom Dictionary

biscotto (Italian for **biscuit**)
- A game that ends in a score that suits both teams, usually a tie game in the group stages of a tournament. The term comes from horse-racing, when horses would be given a biscuit or cookie containing banned substances — to make them either faster or slower — with the purpose of fixing the outcome. ☺

cola de vaca (Spanish for **cow's tail**)
- A trick that involves stopping the ball and then changing direction. Skillful players like Lionel Messi and Gareth Bale are experts at this move, often by keeping the ball close to their instep and leaving their marker behind. 🖐

Fahrstuhlmannschaft (German for **elevator team**)
- A yo-yo team, one that regularly gets relegated and then promoted. ◗◖

brilstand (Dutch for **glasses stand**)
- A goalless game, since 0–0 looks like glasses. ◗◖

Key | ☺ = tactic | **X** = mistake | 🖐 = technique | ◗◖ = team talk *frango* (Brazilian Portuguese for **chicken**)

• One of the most common phrases used in Brazilian soccer, a *frango* is a goal that is the result of an embarrassing mistake by the goalkeeper. **X**

jisatsu-ten (Japanese for **suicide point**)

• An own goal, dating back to when ancient Japanese warriors known as samurai would commit suicide rather than suffer the shame of being captured and tortured by enemies. Part of sportsmanship is that each player on the field takes responsibility for their actions — but nobody dies if they score on their own goalkeeper! ◌◌

hacer un sombrero (Spanish for **to make a hat**)

• Chipping the ball over an opponent's head and running around to retrieve it. ☺ ✍

Alex and Ben's Classroom Dictionary

korokoro (Japanese for **the sound of something rolling slowly across the ground**, like a heavy wheelbarrow pushed across a field or an acorn rolling into a pond)

• A penalty rolled in slowly to the corner where the goalkeeper does not dive. ☺

lanterne rouge (French for **red lantern**)

• The team at the bottom of the standings, named for the last car on a train in France, which has a red light at the back. The same term is used in German: *rote Laterne*. ⊂⊃

Notbremse (German for **emergency brake**)

• A professional foul, when a player deliberately fouls an opponent to prevent a clear goal-scoring opportunity. The punishment is a red card. ☺

pipoqueiro (Brazilian Portuguese for **popcorn seller**)

• A player who avoids taking risks and doesn't play well in important games. ⊂⊃

Key | ☺ = tactic | X = mistake | 🖐 = technique | ⊂⊃ = team talk

saut de grenouille (French for **frog jump**)

• When a player keeps the ball between both feet and jumps over the leg of an opponent. In South America, it is also known as the *Cuauhteminha,* or Blanco Hop, after the Mexican player Cuauhtémoc Blanco, who pulled off the trick in a 1998 World Cup game against South Korea. 🐾

zona Cesarini (Italian for **Cesarini zone**)

• A goal scored in the last few minutes of a game is said to have been scored in the *zona Cesarini* in honor of Juventus winger Renato Cesarini, who scored a very late winning goal for Italy against Hungary in 1931. One week later, Ambrosiana-Inter beat Roma with a late goal, which led the commentator to refer back to the Cesarini goal. The term *zona Cesarini* stuck. 🦉

vuurpijl (Dutch for **rocket**)

• A defensive clearance in which the ball does not go toward the other goal but is hit straight up into the air. 😊

LINGO BINGO

* There are around 7,000 spoken languages today.
* One language dies out every two weeks.
* Languages tend to have from 11 to 210 distinctive sounds. English has about 44.
* There are only 3 vowels in Greenlandic.
* There are around 300 different sign languages.

LYNN GO

⭐ STAR STUDENT

Guten Tag!

Salaam!

Bonjour!

Hi!

¡Hola!

Ciao!

"Bonas paroli!"

(Esperanto for "It's good to talk!")

⭐⭐ STAR STUDENT Stats

Languages spoken: 23
Languages understood: 15
Sign languages learned: ✌
Sign languages understood: 👌
Birthplace: Chatsworth, England
Supports: Seattle Sounders (United States)
Fave player: Michelle French
Trick: Talks a good game

FOREIGN LANGUAGES QUIZ

1. What does the word _Esperanto_ mean in Esperanto?

a) I really gotta pee.
b) One who hopes
c) I like playing soccer.
d) One who speaks ten languages

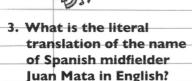

2. Translate this emoji into the most likely sentence:

a) I just swatted a fly.
b) Praise the Lord!
c) Well done!
d) My hands are leaking water.

3. What is the literal translation of the name of Spanish midfielder Juan Mata in English?

a) John Mates
b) John Matters
c) John Kills
d) John Scores

4. In German, if you are _fernweh_, you are:

a) Longing to go to a place far away
b) Full after eating too much food
c) Alone in the woods
d) Always asking too many questions

5. What is the translation of the Italian word _cucchiaio_, used to describe a penalty that is lofted down the middle of the goal?

a) Doughnut
b) Gift
c) Spoon
d) Curly pasta

PHYSICS

A ball is round. Simple!

Well, not really. Professional soccer balls are anything but simple. For a start, they have four parts: **panels of leather** on the outside, a **lining**, a **bladder** inside, and a special tube called a **valve**. (You inflate the ball using a pump and a needle that is stuck through the valve.)

NEEDLE

PUMP

PANELS OF LEATHER

LINING

BLADDER

VALVE

INSIDE A BALL

Second, although they may look it, balls are NOT perfectly round. Their surfaces are actually very uneven. They have seams between the panels and a rough texture on the leather.

In this lesson, we are going to take a closer look at the shape of soccer balls and how they are made to improve play. But first we're going to show you just how far modern balls have come since the time they were made out of pigs' bladders and got so heavy with water it was almost impossible to score a goal from 30 yards/27 meters away.

Oink, oink! Splish, splosh!

ON THE BALL

Here's a roundup of the bounciest facts about balls.

Pigs will fly: The first soccer balls were made from pigs' bladders. Yes, the organ that stores porky pee! Pigs' bladders are light and stretchy and can be inflated with air and then tied, which made them perfectly suited for the job. The bladders were covered with leather so they would keep their shape and not burst when kicked around. The oldest surviving soccer ball is about five hundred years old: it was made from cow leather stitched over a pig's bladder and was discovered at Stirling Castle in Scotland.

Good year for balls: In the mid-nineteenth century, American inventor Charles Goodyear discovered a way to turn latex, a milky substance found in the rubber tree, into hard rubber. In 1855, he made the first soccer ball using rubber: it had rubber panels glued at the seams and was inflated with air. *Boing!*

Best ball: For the 1930 World Cup there was no official ball. South American rivals Uruguay and Argentina faced off in the final, and each wanted to use their own ball. FIFA, the international governing body of soccer, eventually settled the dispute by ruling that the Argentine ball (which was a bit lighter than the Uruguayan ball) would be used in the first half and the Uruguayan ball in the second half. The Argentines won the first half 2–1 with their own ball, but the Uruguayans scored three goals in the second half with their ball, winning the game 4–2. The ball seemed to make all the difference!

To dye for: The first leather balls were brown. In the 1950s, white balls were introduced so that fans could see the ball in floodlit games. In the 1960s, balls were made black and white so they were easier to see on TV. The Premier League now has three types of balls: a white one for the summer, a high-visibility yellow one for the winter, and an orange one for when there is snow.

Heavy stuff: Early balls were held together by stitching and had a slit for an air valve that was sewn up with laces. The tiny holes made by the thread allowed water to enter the ball, making it heavier and harder to kick. Design improvements to the valve meant that soccer balls didn't need the laces anymore. (Some sports, like American football, kept the laces as part of the ball design because they make throwing the ball easier.) Today the panels on a professional soccer ball are held together with a method that bonds them using heat, so they are much less prone to absorbing water.

Wet ball: Cow leather was once used for the ball s outside panels. Today, we use artificial leather, which mimics the feel of leather but absorbs less water. Some balls also have a rough texture that channels the moisture on the surface of the ball so there is more traction when you kick.

PANEL SHOW

The outside skin of a soccer ball is made by attaching identical flat leather panels. When the ball is inflated with air, the panels stretch into a round ball. Here are the three main ways panels are joined. Each is based on a geometric shape.

Cube
Number of panels: 6
It's funny to think that a round ball can be based on a cube! But it can, and they are! Balls used in the 2014 World Cup and Euro 2016 tournaments used six propeller-shaped panels that fit together in a similar way to the square faces of a cube.

Dodecahedron
Number of panels: 12
A dodecahedron is made up of twelve identical pentagons. The 2017–2018 English Premier League ball is based on the dodecahedron.

PROPELLER
PANEL

Truncated icosahedron

Number of sides: 32

The truncated icosahedron is a shape first studied by the ancient Greek mathematician Archimedes more than two thousand years ago, but not for playing ball games! It is made up from twenty hexagons and twelve pentagons. The design became a soccer classic when it was used in the 1970 World Cup.

GLOBAL GLOBES

These are the Men's World Cup balls from 1970 to 2014:

YEAR	HOST COUNTRY	BALL NAME
1970	Mexico	Telstar Durlast
1974	West Germany	Telstar Durlast
1978	Argentina	Tango Durlast
1982	Spain	Tango España
1986	Mexico	Azteca
1990	Italy	Etrusco Unico
1994	United States	Questra
1998	France	Tricolore
2002	Korea/Japan	Fevernova
2006	Germany	Teamgeist
2010	South Africa	Jabulani
2014	Brazil	Brazuca

The 1999 Women's World Cup was played with a specially designed ball called the Icon. Since then, the tournament has been played with the Fevernova (2003), Teamgeist (2007), Speedcell (2011), and Conext15 (2015).

BALL BOOT CAMP

Professional soccer players come in all shapes and sizes. But professional soccer balls must all be the same. Imagine what would happen if the referee showed up with a game ball the size of a pea. Or one as bouncy as a hopper ball. In order to make sure that all professional soccer balls are as similar as possible, FIFA, the international governing body of soccer, requires that all balls pass the following tests:

1. Size (Circumference)

The ball must have a **circumference** (that's the distance all the way around it) of 68.5 to 69.5 centimeters, which is about 27 inches.

The test: The ball is put in a machine that measures the circumference at 4,500 different points.

2. Roundness (Sphericity)

The ball must not deviate by more than 1.5 percent from a perfect sphere, which is the technical term for a perfectly round object.

The test: The same machine that calculates the circumference also calculates how spherical the ball is.

3. Bounce (Rebound)

A ball dropped from 2 meters (6 feet) onto a steel plate must bounce to a height of between 135 and 155 centimeters (4½ to 5 feet).

The test: The ball is placed in a ball-dropping machine, and the bounce is measured ten times.

4. Water absorption

A ball must not absorb more than 10 percent of its weight in water.

The test: The ball is placed in a tank full of water. A robotic arm squashes and turns the ball 250 times in the tank, after which the wet ball is weighed.

5. Weight

The ball must weigh between 420 and 445 grams (about a pound).

The test: The ball is weighed three times in a cabinet protected from the wind.

6. Loss of pressure

Balls are firm because the air inside them pushes the sides out. The force being applied by the air across the inside of the ball is called the **air pressure**.

The ball's pressure must not decrease by more than 20 percent over three days.

The test: The ball is inflated to standard pressure, and its pressure is measured again after seventy-two hours.

7. Shape and size retention

After the ball has been kicked around, the seams and air valve must stay undamaged, the circumference must not change by more than 1.5 percent, its roundness must not deviate by more than 1.5 percent, and its pressure must not change by more than 0.1 bar (1.5 psi).

The test: The ball is measured, then placed in a machine that fires it two thousand times against a steel plate at 50 kilometers (31 miles) per hour, after which it is measured again.

SEAMS LIKE A NICE BALL

As we saw, the leather panels used on balls can be pentagons, hexagons, or propellers. Now let's look at the seams between them. The seams are more than they seem!

The seam helps stop the soccer ball from wobbling all over the place. Here's why. If you have ever played Ping-Pong, you'll know that when you whack the ball, it swerves like crazy. This is because the surface of a Ping-Pong ball is very smooth, and the smoother a ball is, the less predictable its path will be. That's why golf balls are deliberately made with dimples: the dimples stop the ball from wobbling when it is flying through the air.

The same is true of soccer balls. A perfectly round soccer ball would be a nightmare for players and especially goalies, since its path through the air once kicked would be hard to control. The seams in a soccer ball prevent it from veering off course. In the 2010 World Cup, players complained that the tournament's official ball swerved unpredictably when kicked or headed. An investigation into the ball by scientists revealed that its seams were not as deep as those of normal balls, and this was causing its unpredictability. Whoops!

INCREDI-BALL!

It's tradition that players who score a hat trick, or three goals in one game, get to keep the game ball. But what happens if more than one player scores three goals in a game? In that case, the player who completed their hat trick first keeps the ball. That was a pity for Manchester City players Paul Stewart and David White after they beat Huddersfield Town 10–1 in 1987. They both scored hat tricks, but so did Tony Adcock, who got three first and walked off with the ball, before it was whisked away and put in the team's trophy cabinet.

DECCA HEDRON

☆ STAR STUDENT

66See you around!99

☆☆☆ STAR STUDENT Stats

Favorite number: 0
Number of dimples: 12
Number of dimensions: 3
Highest juggling score: 12,000
Birthplace: Cuba
Supports: Ballymena United (Northern Ireland)
Fave player: Kevin Ball
Trick: Great at judging angles

PHYSICS QUIZ

1. For many years soccer balls were made using which part of the pig?

a) Stomach
b) Hooves
c) Buttocks
d) Bladder

2. Before the beginning of every professional game, what does the referee do to the ball?

a) Stands on it to make sure it does not burst
b) Kisses it as part of a ritual
c) Checks the air pressure to make sure it is at the correct level
d) Smells it

3. What happened when a fan of the English team from Liverpool threw a red beach ball onto the field during a 2009 game against Sunderland?

a) One of the Liverpool players headed the ball into the Sunderland goal.
b) The players began an impromptu game of volleyball.

c) The Sunderland striker scored a goal when the real ball rebounded off the beach ball past the Liverpool goalkeeper.
d) A fan in red swimming trunks and a sunhat ran out to retrieve it.

4. What happened when Switzerland midfielder Valon Behrami tackled France's Antoine Griezmann when the countries met each other at the Euro 2016 tournament?

a) The ball burst.
b) The ball flew in Behrami's face and knocked him out.
c) Behrami hid the ball up his shirt.
d) The ball stuck to his shoe.

5. The Nike ball used in the 2016–2017 Premier League Championship was called the:

a) Prestige
b) Catalyst
c) Ordem
d) Strike

FEET FIRST

Soccer is played with your feet. So, if you want to be good at soccer, you need to look after them. And we don't just mean preventing them from smelling! You need strong feet for soccer because when you run, your feet act like levers, propelling your entire body weight forward. When you receive a ball and control it, your feet behave like flexible shock absorbers.

In the first after-school club of the week, we have four exercises for our feet and ankles that will help toughen up these five-toed trotters. You can even do these in your bedroom, so no excuses. Now, best foot forward!

Exercise 1:
Balancing stick

Stand on a flat surface on one leg with your raised knee bent for 10 seconds. Look at a fixed point on the wall to help you focus. Your hands should be on your hips or hanging by your sides. Then do it with your eyes closed. Then switch legs. As you get better, change the surface you're standing on from a flat floor to a sofa cushion to something wobbly. And when you get good, try staying balanced for 30 seconds.

GOOD FOR: Muscle strength and training the brain
DIFFICULTY RATING: 1/4

Exercise 2: Heel ordeal

Stand on tiptoes. Hold for 5 seconds, then lower to your heels. Repeat 5 times.

GOOD FOR: Strengthening muscles at the back of the leg and foot
DIFFICULTY RATING: 2/4

What a bummer!

Exercise 3: Bum ankles

Put your bare feet together and squat so your bottom touches your ankles. Start by holding the squat for 10 seconds, and then gradually increase to 30 seconds.

GOOD FOR: General mobility, which requires strong ankles
DIFFICULTY RATING: 3/4

Exercise 4: Toes up

Take off your shoes and socks. Push your big toe down on the floor while pushing the other toes up into the air. No hands allowed! This stretches or flexes your ligaments. Start by holding the stretch for 10 seconds, and then gradually increase to 30 seconds. Don't forget to switch feet.

GOOD FOR: Pushing off strongly in sprints
DIFFICULTY RATING: 4/4

FOOT NOTE! Only do what feels comfortable to you. Do not exceed the stated time in each exercise, as you could be at risk of injury.

Today girls play soccer at school and dream of becoming professional players and having the chance to win the World Cup.

There is a professional women's league in the United States and in countries like France, Germany, and Sweden. But this was not always the case. Until the final years of the nineteenth century, hardly any women played soccer.

This was why in 1894 Nettie Honeyball placed a newspaper ad asking for women to join her in founding the British Ladies' Football Club. You might have thought that with a name like Nettie Honeyball, she was destined to love the game! However, Nettie wasn't the woman's real name. She wanted her identity to stay secret, probably because the idea of women's soccer at that time was so scandalous.

The British Ladies' Football Club lasted only a couple of years. But two decades later, women's soccer became a phenomenon! In this lesson we are going to look at the moment in history when women's soccer was more popular than men's soccer. It happened in Great Britain at a time when women were demanding the same opportunities as men. At Soccer School we think women and men should have equal opportunities—on and off the field.

And here are my teammates, Pen Altie, Suzie Scissor-Kick, and Maisie Dribble.

SOCCER FACTORY

In 1914, the First World War began. Britain and France were
at war with Germany, and in the following years several
million British men were sent to fight in France. Soon there
weren't enough men in Britain to do lots of essential jobs,
particularly physical ones. Traditionally,
women were expected to stay
at home and look after the
children and the house
and do domestic chores
like cooking and
cleaning. But during
the war, women
stepped in to help
out and took
on new roles such as:

- ⚽ Delivering mail
- ⚽ Factory work
- ⚽ Farming
- ⚽ Fishing
- ⚽ Making weapons
- ⚽ Teaching in boys' schools

One place that hired lots of women during
the First World War was Dick, Kerr and Company, a
factory in Lancashire owned by W. B. Dick and John Kerr.
The factory usually made streetcars but during the war
switched to making bombs and bullets. The mixture of
male and female workers was new for everyone and had
an unexpected consequence: one day in 1917, the men
challenged the women to a soccer game.

A soccer game involving women was an extraordinary idea at that time, since women just didn't play soccer. But since there was a war on and women were doing the same jobs as men, it seemed reasonable that women should join in with soccer too.

The game was so fun for the women that they decided to carry on playing together. Later that year, they organized a charity soccer game to raise money for the local hospital that was caring for wounded soldiers. They wanted to play against another team of women, so they asked a group of women at another factory nearby.

The game took place on Christmas Day, 1917: Dick, Kerr's Ladies, as they now called themselves, played Arundel Coulthard Foundry. The venue was Deepdale, the stadium of Preston North End, the local professional soccer team. It had been lying unused because of the war. The game was a huge success. About ten thousand people came to watch and a lot of money was raised for the hospital.

That pass was a gift!

LADIES' GAME

The game sparked a boom in women's soccer. Dick, Kerr's Ladies began to play more games farther afield, and thousands of spectators flocked to watch. Other women's teams started up too. Factory owners were eager for their female workers to play since it boosted spirits and was healthy and cheap entertainment.

Even when the First World War ended, on November 11, 1918, women's soccer continued to spread, and Dick, Kerr's Ladies became famous as the best team in the country, rarely losing a game. Their games were always well attended, and in 1919 when they traveled to play Newcastle United Ladies, thirty-five thousand people filled the stands!

Dick, Kerr's players wore the same uniform as the men's team — soccer shoes, long socks, shorts, and a jersey of black-and-white vertical stripes — as well as small striped hats to cover their hair. The women quickly became celebrities and an inspiration to countless other women.

On December 26, 1920, Dick, Kerr's Ladies played their archrivals, Saint Helens Ladies, in Liverpool. The stadium was packed with fifty-three thousand fans and another fourteen thousand couldn't get in. It was the biggest crowd Liverpool had ever seen. The players needed a police escort to get to the locker rooms.

By now, the Dick, Kerr's Ladies team had a schedule as if they were professional players, playing an average of two games a week for nine months of the year. In 1920, they played the first women's international game, against France at Deepdale, in front of a crowd of twenty-five thousand. Later that year, they played in France. In 1921 alone, the team played sixty-seven games.

But they were not professionals, receiving only paid time off to play and reimbursement for game expenses. The women still worked at the factory and even did a shift before midweek games. They were the hardest-working soccer players in the country!

STADIUM BAN

You might have thought that the success of women's soccer would be applauded by the English Football Association, especially since the games were for charity. But the FA did not like it at all. The women were attracting bigger crowds than the men's professional league, which had restarted in 1919 after the war.

At the end of 1921, the FA passed a ruling saying that clubs were not allowed to use their stadiums for women's soccer. "The council feel impelled to express their strong opinion that the game of soccer is quite unsuitable for females and ought not to be encouraged," it said. The ruling was a devastating blow, as it left the women's teams with no decent-size stadiums to play in. Even though teams like Dick, Kerr's Ladies carried on, only a few fans could watch them play, and most women's teams were forgotten by the public.

Despite the ruling, in 1922 Dick, Kerr's Ladies went on tour to the United States, playing to crowds of up to ten thousand. One newspaper wrote:

> The Dick, Kerr team is one of the biggest things in soccer to have visited the United States.

It took until 1971 for the FA to lift its ban on clubs allowing women's soccer. And since then, women's soccer has started to grow again with the first Women's World Cup held in 1991.

WONDER WOMAN

One reason that Dick, Kerr's Ladies almost never lost a game was because they had the best player of that generation. Lily Parr (1905–1978) was from Merseyside

CRACK!

Goodness gracious!

and learned to play soccer with her older brothers. She joined Dick, Kerr's as a winger when she was just fourteen years old—and scored forty-three goals in her first season! Parr was

KAPOW!

famed for her power and aggressive playing style. At six feet/183 centimeters tall, she towered over her teammates. According to one story, she once kicked a ball so hard it broke a male goalkeeper's arm when he tried to catch it.

Parr went on playing soccer for Dick, Kerr's Ladies after the FA ban. She continued playing for the team when it later changed its name to Preston Ladies, only retiring in 1951, when her career goal tally stood at more than nine hundred. She is considered the best female soccer player of all time and in 2002 was the first woman to be inducted into the English Football Hall of Fame at the National Football Museum in England.

ON A PAR WITH LILY

We think these three rank with Lily Parr as the best players of all time:

Mia Hamm (United States)

The forward made her debut for the United States at just fifteen years old and went on to score 158 goals in 275 national team appearances. She won two World Cups and two Olympic gold medals. Hamm co-owns the American team Los Angeles FC and is a board member of the Italian club Roma.

Marta (Brazil)

The Brazilian forward won five consecutive FIFA World Player of the Year Awards (2006–2010) and is the Women's World Cup's all-time leading goal scorer. She averages more than a goal per game for Brazil—and has played more than a hundred games!

Sun Wen (China)

The former China captain was voted FIFA's Female Player of the Century after winning four Asian Cups and playing in four World Cups and two Olympics. She was top scorer and best player in the 1999 Women's World Cup.

EQUAL RIGHTS

When Dick, Kerr's Ladies started playing soccer, they were showing that women could do something traditionally thought of as just being for men. At that time in history, men and women had very different roles in society. Women were seen mostly as homemakers, raising children, serving their husbands, and making sure domestic life was well run. Men worked outside the home and earned a wage.

But there were other differences too between the roles and status of men and women. Perhaps the most controversial difference was that only men were allowed to vote.

In the years before the First World War, some women were so outraged that they were not allowed to take part in elections that they began to campaign for the right to vote. In 1848, women gathered in Seneca Falls, New York, for the first women's rights convention, and in 1903,

Emmeline Pankhurst founded a movement called the Women's Social and Political Union, one of several that campaigned in Great Britain at that time. Some activists for these movements—known as **suffragettes**, since the word *suffrage* means the right to vote—used violent techniques like smashing windows of public buildings and setting fire to them, and chaining themselves to railings to draw attention to the cause. When they were arrested by the police, they went on hunger strikes in prison, meaning they refused to eat.

When the First World War began in 1914, many suffragettes stopped their campaigning in order to help with the war effort. In 1918, the same year the war ended, the British government gave the vote to women over the age of thirty, in part thanks to the vital role women played during the war by taking over men's roles. Two years later, women in the United States were also granted the right to vote, after more than fifty years of protests.

SHE'S IN CHARGE

More than fifty countries have now had women as their elected leaders, including:

COUNTRY	LEADER	POSITION	DATES
Argentina	Cristina Kirchner	President	2007–2015
Australia	Julia Gillard	Prime Minister	2010–2013
Brazil	Dilma Rousseff	President	2011–2016
Germany	Angela Merkel	Chancellor	from 2005
India	Indira Gandhi	Prime Minister	1966–1977, 1980–1984
United Kingdom	Margaret Thatcher	Prime Minister	1979–1990
United Kingdom	Theresa May	Prime Minister	from 2016

SUE FRIDGE

☆ STAR STUDENT

VOTE 4 ME

66 Fair play for all! 99

☆☆☆ STAR STUDENT Stats

Number of votes: 12 million
Number of sisters: 4
Number of striped hats: 22
Orders taken from men: 0
Birthplace: Sisteron, France
Supports: Orlando Pride (United States)
Fave referee: Graham Poll
Trick: Always wins team votes

HISTORY QUIZ

1. During the First World War, why did women start to do many of the jobs traditionally done by men?

a) Because women are better than men

b) Because many men had joined the army to fight

c) Because men wanted companionship at work

d) Because women got better grades on their exams

2. If you play soccer, but do not get paid for it, what type of player are you?

a) Not very good

b) Semiprofessional

c) Poor

d) Amateur

3. What is a foundry?

a) A factory that casts metal

b) A factory that uses material found on the street

c) A place where you go to dry clothes

d) A cheese shop

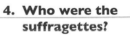

4. Who were the suffragettes?

a) Women who campaigned for the right to vote

b) Female fans from Suffolk

c) The name given to the female supporters of a losing team

d) A girl band

5. Which team has won the Women's World Cup the most times?

a) Germany

b) Japan

c) Norway

d) USA

BOTANY

F ields have changed in many ways since 1863, when the rules of soccer were first written down:

> ⚽ The maximum length of a field used to be 200 yards/ 183 meters. Today it is 115 yards/105 meters.
> ⚽ Originally there were no markings for the penalty spot, the penalty box, the D, the halfway line, or the center circle.
> ⚽ Goals used to be just two upright posts. Then a tape was hung between the posts. Later a crossbar was introduced, and later still a net was added to avoid doubt over scored goals.

One thing, however, has stayed the same: the surface of the field. Soccer has always been played on grass.

In this lesson, we are going to discover why grass is one of the most amazing plants in the world. Not only is grass crucial to soccer and many other sports; it has also changed the course of civilization.

Weed on!

GRASS IS CLASS

Grass is one of the oldest types of plant. Scientists think it was growing around one hundred million years ago, during the age of the dinosaurs, because they found five types of grass in a dinosaur's fossilized poop. Stinky business!

🐝 All grasses have similar characteristics. They all have a hollow stem and usually leaves, or blades, that are long and thin and relatively rigid. Some grass leaves are so sharp, they can cut human skin.

🐝 Grass comes in many varieties. There are about ten thousand species, including short grass, which we use on lawns, and long grass, which can grow higher than a house.

🐝 Grasses are long-lived. Some species of grass can live for hundreds of years.

🐝 Grass is versatile. It will grow on pretty much every habitat on Earth, including hot deserts, rain forests, and cold mountains.

🐝 Grass is everywhere! You will find it on all the world's continents, even Antarctica. In fact, up to 40 percent of all the land in the world is covered in grass.

GRAZE CRAZE

Some of the most common foods we eat are grasses, such as wheat, corn, rice, and oats. We eat the seeds of these grasses, which we call **grains**. In fact, the discovery that we could grow grasses for their grains marked the moment that some humans stopped being hunter-gatherers, moving from place to place, looking for food. Instead, many people became farmers, based in the same place, tending fields and storing grains for use all year round. This was the beginning of villages, towns, and eventually cities.

HUMAN EATS EVERYTHING

COW EATS GRASS

GRASS

FOOD CHAIN

Animals like cows, horses, sheep, and deer are grass eaters too. In fact, the word *graze*, which we use to describe how these animals eat, means "to eat grass."

This means that grass is an important food for humans in two ways: first as something for us to eat, and second as something for the animals that we eat to eat. The process by which plants (such as grass) are eaten by animals (such as cows) that in turn are eaten by other animals (such as humans) is called a **food chain**.

MULTI-GRASSING
Bread comes from wheat, which is a grass, and sugar comes from sugarcane, which is also a grass. So if you are having a sandwich and some orange soda while watching a soccer game, you are eating, drinking, and watching grass at the same time!

ONE MAN WENT TO MOW . . .

Grass isn't just for eating. In the form of lawns, it has become an essential part of people's yards. Ben loves mowing the lawn on weekends, although his rows tend to be a bit wonky. Alex's are much straighter! The first lawns were grassy fields that surrounded English castles; they were kept short either by cattle grazing on them or by workers who used sharp-bladed tools called scythes. The grass had to be kept short so enemies could be spotted approaching the castle.

By the 1800s, having a grass lawn around your house had become a sign of wealth, because you could only have a lawn on your land if you were able to pay workers to cut it with scythes. Using a scythe was slow and laborious work, and a big lawn required a team of scythe wielders. Expensive!

But all this changed thanks to Edwin Beard Budding, an inventor who was asked by a clothing factory to find a way of cutting off all the tufty bits of cloth from soldiers' uniforms. He invented a machine with a rotating device that cut off the tufts. He realized his invention could work on grass . . . and in 1830, he invented the lawn mower.

The lawn mower made it cheaper and easier to maintain a lawn. The Budding Mower became a bestseller and changed our yards forever.

... WENT TO MOW A MEADOW

One of the loudest songs sung at the English team Chelsea's games is the children's nursery rhyme "One Man Went to Mow." Fans think it was introduced by a Chelsea fan named Mickey Greenaway, who played a nursery rhyme tape of the song while Chelsea was playing a friendly match in Sweden in 1981. Chelsea fans all sang along and eventually the chant became a tradition.

One man went to mow . . .

SPORTING PLANTS

Grass is different from other plants because the leaves grow from the bottom of the stem. This means it can withstand being eaten from the top and also being trampled on. It is this resistance that makes it perfect for soccer fields. Unlike other plants, it doesn't die when it's stomped on.

Even though the blades of some grasses can be really sharp, other species are very soft. Softer grasses are ideal for sports, as the plant will act as a cushion when players fall. Even the best artificial soccer fields are not as soft as a well-tended grass field.

TURF WAR

Just as English castle owners hired people to maintain their lawns, so do soccer teams. Soccer fields require a lot of attention to be at their best. We wanted to find out more, so we visited a team with a cutting-edge reputation and the man who has helped make it.

Leicester City in England surprised everyone when they won the 2015–2016 Premier League title. It wasn't the only award they took home that season, though: because of the incredible field at their King Power Stadium and the fields at their training ground, the team won Professional Football Grounds Team of the Year. We can only imagine the shear delight! The grounds team celebrated by mowing diamond shapes into the field on the final day of the season, with a star inside each diamond. It was a perfectly symmetrical pattern and celebrated the double success in style. "It was like drawing a big dot-to-dot picture," the head grounds manager, John Ledwidge, told us.

Ledwidge wanted to mow an image of the Champions League ball into the center circle before European games, but that was forbidden by UEFA, the European governing body. They say that for Champions League games, the grass has to be mowed in straight lines. Ledwidge is always coming up with wacky design ideas. He might even mow the Soccer School crest into our field if we ask nicely!

GREEN FINGERS

Ledwidge's skill is in creating patterns even though grass is just one color: green. He can shade the green by mowing the grass in different directions: grass bent away from the mower will appear lighter, and grass bent toward the mower will appear darker. He gets deeper contrasts between the greens by using a roller, which flattens the grass even more. "We try to be as creative as we can within the framework of only using dark green and light green," he says. "We are all mad scientists, really!"

This field is a cut above!

In order to create the perfect field, every day Ledwidge puts a stick called a moisture probe about 6 inches/15 centimeters under the surface to check moisture levels. The probe contains sensors that tell him how much water the grass needs that day. In other words, he is asking the grass how thirsty it is.

Every month, he also takes soil samples to check the levels of nutrients. So he's asking how hungry the grass is! Ledwidge then creates a special mixture, based on what he discovers, to spray on the grass.

In summer the grass needs more water to keep it hydrated—just like a player—while in winter it needs **nutrients** like iron and potassium to strengthen it. Ledwidge even adds liquefied sugar and seaweed to the spray to keep the grass healthy. Supposedly, Manchester City puts garlic in their grass spray. Not good if a team of vampires ever plays there!

LEDWIDGE'S GREAT GRASS FACTS

In summer we can mow the field up to three times per day.

About 2,000 quarts/1,900 liters of paint is used every year to mark the fields (seven fields at the training ground and one at the stadium).

We walk 7½ miles/12 kilometers every time we mow the field.

FIELD GOOD

We see the grass on top of the field, but this is what's happening below it:

GRASS
1 inch/2.5 centimeters
For playing soccer on!

SYNTHETIC GRASS
7 inches/18 centimeters
Fake grass made of synthetic fibers is stitched into a mixture of sand and soil. This helps bind the grass roots.

PURE SAND
8 inches/20 centimeters
To help drainage and prevent waterlogging as the water moves down from the grass to the roots.

GRAVEL CARPET
Contains pipes for draining away the water.

HOW DOES YOUR GARDEN GROW?

The length of grass on a sports field depends on what you want the object in the sport to do. For example, in rugby the ball does not touch the ground, so the grass will be longer than in other sports.

Some sports need even longer grass:

SPORTS FIELD	GRASS LENGTH (MM)
Cricket wicket	0
Golf putting green	2–3 mm
Bowling green	4.5 mm
Tennis court	1/2 in./10 mm
Soccer field	1 in./30 mm
Rugby field	2 in./50 mm
Horse racing track	2½ in./60 mm

LORNE MOWER

STAR STUDENT

66 Turf guys come first! 99

STAR STUDENT Stats

Thickness of hair: 2 in./5 cm
Daily water intake: a gallon
Rotary blade power: 100 w
Longest rendition of "One Man Went to Mow": 84 men
Birthplace: Grasse, France
Supports: Grasshopper Club Zürich (Switzerland)
Favorite Player: Rob Green
Trick: Cutting it close

BOTANY QUIZ

1. What grass-related song do Chelsea fans sing?

a) "The Green, Green Grass of Home"

b) "One Man Went to Mow"

c) "Green Grass Grows All Around"

d) "How Does the Grass Grow?"

2. Why is grass green?

a) It's not. It's blue!

b) The sun paints it green every night.

c) So grasshoppers can jump around without being seen

d) Grass produces a pigment called chlorophyll, which reflects green light.

3. Rotting plants are eaten by flies, which are eaten by spiders, which are eaten by mice, which are eaten by foxes. What might eat a fox in this food chain?

a) A duck-billed platypus

b) A fly

c) A unicorn

d) A bear

4. Which country's league introduced a rule in 2016 saying the grass needed to be greener in order to appeal more to fans and sponsors?

a) Spain

b) Russia

c) China

d) Greenland

5. What was unique about the lawn mower that English lower-league team Forest Green Rovers started using in 2012?

a) The players built it from scratch.

b) It was solar powered and used by a robot.

c) The manager's eight-year-old son was hired to mow the field.

d) It painted field markings at the same time.

FILM STUDIES

Which team usually gets to the stadium the day before a soccer game?

The TV crew!

When we sit down in front of the TV to watch a big game, we expect to see every important moment. We want to see every goal from different angles. We also want to see close-ups of the players' and coaches' faces, as well as wide shots of the whole team. That's a lot of work for a TV crew.

In fact, a ninety-minute televised game is in many ways like a ninety-minute movie. They are both full of dazzling and dramatic images, in glorious color and high definition, and they both need a lot of technical preparation.

In today's lesson, we're going to learn how a game of soccer is filmed for television.

Lights! Camera! Action!

HIGH TECH

Here's a list of the basic equipment a television company needs to televise a soccer game:

- TV cameras
- Cables
- TV screens
- Computers
- A truck

A truck? Yes! You'll see why very soon.

All the cameras, cables, and computers usually arrive at the stadium the day before the game, along with a team of about thirty people. These include **technicians**, whose job is to set up the equipment, and a team of other technical specialists who make sure everything is working properly.

That's right. The TV cameras are not owned by the team or kept in the stadium. They must be set up by the TV company from scratch each time.

The technicians put the cameras in their correct positions around the field. They then connect cables between each camera and the truck, which is parked in the stadium parking lot. The truck opens up to become a TV studio, containing screens and computers for the technical team who will control the **broadcast** of the game on television.

It takes at least three hours to fully set up and check the equipment. Sometimes it can take up to twelve hours. It's an exhausting day, and the game hasn't even started!

COLOR BALANCE

One of the crucial jobs on the day before the game is to make sure the cameras are all seeing the same colors. If you ever take several pictures of the same thing from different angles, such as, say, a pair of red socks, you will notice that the red can look totally different in each image. This is because the light is different in each picture.

The same thing happens with TV cameras in a soccer stadium—the green of the field looks different under different lights. Since the lighting changes with every camera position, each of the cameras needs to have its **color balance** adjusted so they are all the same. It would look very strange if one camera showed the grass as dark green, another as lime green, and another as olive green.

YES, WE CAM

This is a camera plan for a typical big game.

You'll notice that almost all the main cameras are on one side of the field. That's because the viewer needs to always be clear which team is playing in which direction. If a team is playing from left to right, the images need to show them

CAMERA PLAN

UPPER-DECK CAMERAS

1. **CAMERA 1:** The main camera, on the midfield line, which provides 60 to 70 percent of all images. Gives a wide view of the game.
2. **CAMERA 2:** Next to Camera 1, but used for close-up shots.
3. **& 4. 18-YARD CAMERAS:** In line with the edge of the box. Both of these cameras are useful for checking offside calls.

FIELDSIDE CAMERAS

5. **CAMERA 3:** Used for player and referee close-ups. When a player is fouled, Camera 3 shoots the player on the ground, while Camera 2 shoots the player who committed the foul.
6. **& 7. 6-YARD CAMERAS:** In line with the box markings, for getting goalmouth action.

playing from left to right. A camera on the opposite side would have them playing right to left, which would be very confusing for the viewer!

Each camera below is operated by someone—some are right up close to the action, and some are high up at the back of the stands on a metal walkway called a **gantry** or **upper deck**.

SIDE AND STAND CAMERAS
8. COACH CAM: Watching the coaches and the benches.
9. & 10. HIGH BEHIND-GOAL CAMERAS
11. & 12. CORNER CAMERAS: These give you extra angles for replays.
13. BEAUTY CAM: A wide-angle camera that is used to get a beautiful shot of the stadium (perhaps with the sun setting).

ON THE MOVE

The cameras in the diagram are the cameras that are fixed in one location. But TV networks use other cameras too — ones that move around.

STEADY ON

If you want to film the teams as they walk out from the locker room onto the field, you need to walk with them. If you want close-up shots of players celebrating on the field as soon as the final whistle blows, you need to be as close as possible to them. In both of these situations, the film crew uses a **Steadicam**.

A Steadicam is a portable camera that is carried using a special harness. You often see Steadicam operators running around in the middle of the action: the camera is on a stick, which is connected to an arm, which is connected to the harness.

Camera operators need a harness to hold the camera because the equipment is heavy. The harness spreads the weight evenly across the operator's back, shoulders, and hips, helping keep the camera as steady as possible when they move.

If you have ever tried to film something on a phone or a camera, you know that you have to keep your hands as still as possible, since images from a shaky camera are hard to watch. Steadicams are designed to stop camera wobble. Think about what happens when you try to walk while holding a glass of water full to the brim. In order to stop the water from spilling, you must constantly adjust your arm so that it absorbs the bounce of your walk. Steadicams work on the same principle: the equipment is like a robot arm that will absorb the bounce of your walk, and will keep the camera steady and moving in a fluid motion.

It takes about forty minutes for a Steadicam operator to get ready, which is mostly spent making sure the weight of the camera and equipment is perfectly balanced on the harness. Altogether the equipment weighs 50 pounds / 23 kilograms—about the same as a large dog!

Steadicam operators always have an assistant beside them. The Steadicam operator uses one hand to control the direction of the camera and the other hand to adjust the zoom. The assistant controls the focus, using a dial on a handset. And the assistant also makes sure the operator doesn't accidentally bump into anyone behind them. Eek!

DRONE ON

Some televised games use a remote-controlled camera fixed to a **drone**, a remote-controlled flying machine with four propellers. The camera hovers above the stadium to get bird's-eye views. The camera needs two people to operate it: one for the drone (who must have a drone flying license) and one for the camera itself.

Holy flying camera, Batman!

BIRD'S-EYE VIEW

Another way to get overhead shots is to use a **Skycam**. Two cables are hung diagonally across the field, each one hanging between two opposite corners. The Skycam is placed where the two cables cross each other. Operators tighten or loosen the cables at the four corners of the field, and make the Skycam move in three directions: lengthwise across the field, widthwise across the field, and higher or lower to cover the action from different heights.

MEANWHILE, IN THE PARKING LOT

The stadium parking lot does not sound like a particularly interesting place to be while a game is going on, but in fact it is a hive of excitement and activity.

The truck we mentioned earlier has been transformed into a TV studio, full of screens and computers, with space inside for about twenty people.

The most important person in the truck is the **director**, who is sitting in front of a wall of screens that show all the images coming in from the cameras.

The director's job is to choose which of these images is used in the broadcast. Most of the time, the image used will be the overview given by the main camera, Camera 1. But the director needs to be aware of the images coming from all the cameras, in case there is a better view of the action at any moment.

The director wears headphones and a microphone, which are connected to all the camera operators' headsets. Often the director talks to the camera operators, asking them to get certain shots.

Also in the truck are other members of the broadcast team, such as the people handling the sound, the graphics, and the replays. Film crews have lots of special words for things, such as *chyron* (pronounced KĪ ron), which is the term for a caption used on the lower third of the screen.

ONE MORE TIME

One reason sports like soccer are so popular on TV is the ability to show replays. We love reliving the best moments again and again. But the first viewers to ever see an instant replay in sports were not so happy. The replay was shown on a channel in the United States in 1963 during a game of American football. When one team scored a touchdown, the channel replayed the moment and the announcer had to make clear that the team was not scoring again. Many viewers were confused and called the channel to complain!

UNPUNCTUAL GERMANS

The first game of the Bundesliga—the top German division—took place in August 1963. Borussia Dortmund was playing Werder Bremen. Only one TV camera was in the stadium. But the cameraman arrived late, and when Dortmund striker Friedhelm Konietzka scored after only thirty-five seconds, no one was there to film it. This means there is no footage of the first ever Bundesliga goal. Embarrassing, *ja*!

DON'T MISS IT

When England captain Steven Gerrard scored in his team's 2010 World Cup opening game against the United States, the whole country celebrated. Except, that is, for the thousands of people who missed the goal because one of the TV channels that was showing the game cut to a car ad by mistake. Oops!

The channel had made the same mistake one year earlier, switching to ads with two minutes of overtime left to play of a goalless English FA Cup tie between Everton and Liverpool. While viewers were watching an ad for mints, Everton scored a last-minute winner. But all viewers saw was the players celebrating afterward.

KE-OWWWWWW-N

Often TV pundits and presenters stand on the side of the field before games and set the scene for the game ahead. One former player was in for a nasty surprise while assessing the pregame form of English teams Leeds United and Arsenal before an FA Cup tie in 2012. A ball from the field smashed him on the head while he was chatting on live TV. Ouch!

The victim, Martin Keown, a former Arsenal defender, did not look pleased. Keown later claimed that the shot had been struck by Leeds midfielder Michael Brown—who had once played for Arsenal's rivals, the Spurs—and that Brown had apparently been aiming for the man standing next to Keown, Robbie Savage!

"SLOW" MO REPLAY

★ STAR
☆ STUDENT

66 What a shot! 99

★★ STAR
☆ STUDENT Stats

Number of cameras: 23
Length of cables: 5 miles/8 km
Toy trucks: 14
Prematch buildup: 20 mins.
Birthplace: River Cam, England
Supports: Aldershot Town (U.K.)
Fave player: Geoff Cameron
Trick: Amazing focus

FILM STUDIES QUIZ

1. What is the name of the raised platform where the main cameras are placed?

a) The garret
b) The gantry
c) The pantry
d) The tree

2. The first game broadcast live on TV was on September 16, 1937. The game was between:

a) Arsenal and Arsenal Reserves
b) Manchester United and Liverpool
c) England and Scotland
d) Brazil and Argentina

3. Who decides which pictures will be used on TV?

a) The producer
b) The director
c) The decider
d) The viewer

4. In 2013, Argentine player Ezequiel Lavezzi, playing for Paris Saint-Germain, walked off the field after a hard-fought game against rivals Marseille. What joke did he play on the Steadicam operator?

a) Made faces at him
b) Chased him
c) Covered his camera
d) Tripped him up

5. There are about 7.5 billion people in the world. How many of them watched at least a minute of the 2014 World Cup final between Germany and Argentina on TV?

a) About half a billion
b) About one billion
c) About two billion
d) About three billion

BRAIN GAME

It's a World Cup final. The world is watching and your team has a penalty kick that could win the trophy. The captain gives you the ball to take the kick. What happens next? Will you stay calm, or let your nerves get the better of you? We all face moments of pressure in our lives, whether we're performing in public or taking a test. Soccer players are no different. In this second after-school club, we have some ways to mentally prepare you for your next tough challenge. Focus!

Challenge 1: Knees up

When you get dressed in the morning, tie your shoelaces while standing on one leg. Not only is this task good for muscles and balance, it is also good for coping with mental pressure. We are not used to standing on one leg, so this challenge helps us get comfortable with being uncomfortable. If we are not afraid of being uncomfortable, we are likely to perform much better when the heat is on!

Kneesie does it!

GOOD FOR: Keeping cool under pressure
TIME COMMITMENT: 1/3

Challenge 2: Brilliant me

Get a piece of paper and write down some times you've done well at school or in sports or helped out at home. Also write down nice things that teachers, friends, and family members have said to you. Put it somewhere safe. This document will help you feel good about yourself. If you ever have a bad day, look at the piece of paper to remind yourself of all your successes. In sports and in life, it is important to believe in yourself. Players who do will keep trying to succeed even if they sometimes fail.

GOOD FOR: Recovering from setbacks
TIME COMMITMENT: 2/3

Challenge 3: Check it out

Memorize this checklist.

This list was written by a soccer psychologist for players, to ensure that they are continually progressing in their careers. That's because the best players never think they know everything. The same goes for your teachers and even the Soccer School coaches. We are always learning! The checklist is a useful reminder of ways to make progress both on and off the field.

1. Identify areas you want to improve.

2. Set small, achievable goals.

3. Look ahead, not back; you can't change the past.

GOOD FOR: Staying motivated
TIME COMMITMENT: 3/3

ENGINEERING

S tadiums are buildings where soccer games take place in front of spectators. But, of course, they are much more than that! They are often enormous, towering structures that dominate the skylines of their cities. In fact, we think they are a bit like modern-day castles. A stadium, like a castle, strikes fear into the hearts of enemies. A stadium prominently displays its team colors, just as a castle displays flags. And let's not forget the army of fans who treat the stadium as a home and protect its honor by waving banners and scarves and cheering at every game. The most famous stadiums, such as Wembley in London, San Siro in Milan, and Camp Nou in Barcelona, are known throughout the world.

In this lesson, we are going to find out how stadiums are built so both the players and fans get the most out of a game. We're going to visit some amazing structures and discover some naughty tricks home teams use to upset the visiting team.

But first, something sick.

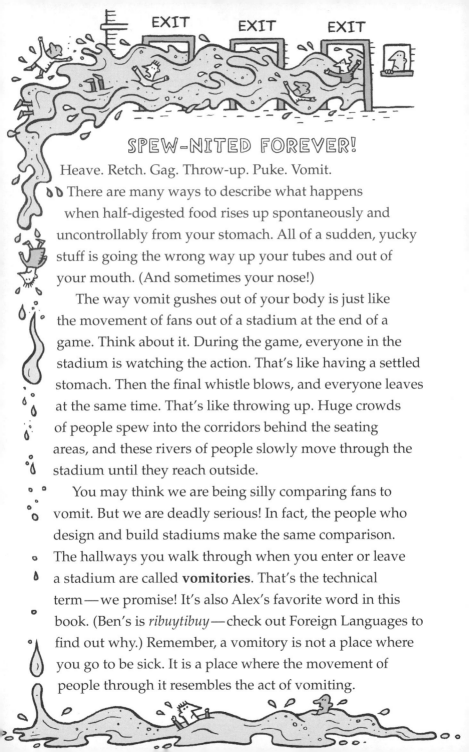

SPEW-NITED FOREVER!

Heave. Retch. Gag. Throw-up. Puke. Vomit.
There are many ways to describe what happens when half-digested food rises up spontaneously and uncontrollably from your stomach. All of a sudden, yucky stuff is going the wrong way up your tubes and out of your mouth. (And sometimes your nose!)

The way vomit gushes out of your body is just like the movement of fans out of a stadium at the end of a game. Think about it. During the game, everyone in the stadium is watching the action. That's like having a settled stomach. Then the final whistle blows, and everyone leaves at the same time. That's like throwing up. Huge crowds of people spew into the corridors behind the seating areas, and these rivers of people slowly move through the stadium until they reach outside.

You may think we are being silly comparing fans to vomit. But we are deadly serious! In fact, the people who design and build stadiums make the same comparison. The hallways you walk through when you enter or leave a stadium are called **vomitories**. That's the technical term—we promise! It's also Alex's favorite word in this book. (Ben's is *ribuytibuy*—check out Foreign Languages to find out why.) Remember, a vomitory is not a place where you go to be sick. It is a place where the movement of people through it resembles the act of vomiting.

CROWD CONTROL

If you have ever visited a stadium, you'll know that
walking through a vomitory at the end of a game can be
a bit scary. You will be in a crowd of thousands of people,
who are all moving the same way at the same time. There is
no way to go faster. There is no way to go backward. There
is nothing you can do to escape. All you can do is walk
slowly in the same direction as everyone else.

Because of the risks of fans causing a stampede, or a
crush, as they leave the stadium, **architects**, the people who
design and plan buildings, say that the vomitories are one
of the most crucial parts of stadium design. If the hallways
are too narrow, you will get squashed. But if they are too
big, you are wasting space that could be used for things
that fans need, such as toilets, and things that make the
team money, such as food stands.

Safety guidelines in the U.K. require stadiums to be
designed so that it is possible to get everyone out of the
stands in eight minutes. That's not a lot of time
to get about sixty thousand people out.
Sometimes it takes Ben longer
than that to get out of bed
in the morning!

ANY SPARE TICKETS?

Most major stadiums are built to hold tens of thousands of fans. But when safety regulations were less strict about the number of people allowed, some games attracted more than a hundred thousand spectators, which is about equal to the population of a medium-size town! Here are the highest confirmed attendances from our favorite moments in soccer history:

173,850

Stadium: Maracanã, Rio de Janeiro, Brazil

A world-record crowd was left heartbroken as Brazil lost 2–1 to Uruguay in the 1950 World Cup final. Unofficial estimates claim that attendance might have topped two hundred thousand.

147,365

Stadium: Hampden Park, Glasgow, Scotland

Fans poured into Scotland's biggest stadium at the time to see Celtic beat Aberdeen 2–1 in the 1937 Scottish Cup final.

128,000

Stadium: Azadi, Tehran, Iran

Iran drew 1–1 with Australia in the 1998 World Cup qualifying playoff in front of a packed home crowd. Iran ended up qualifying for its first World Cup since 1978.

126,047

Stadium: Wembley, London, England

Bolton Wanderers beat West Ham United 2–0 in the 1923 FA Cup final, the first ever official game at Wembley. But it's remembered for a gray horse named Billie shepherding the crowds to safety.

STAND UP, SIT DOWN

The section of the stadium where spectators watch the game is called the **stands**, which is totally confusing since spectators nowadays spend most of the time in the stands sitting down. Go figure!

An architect's job when designing the stands is to give as many people as possible a good view of the action on the field. The reason stadiums are all different is that architects have several other factors to take into account, such as how much money there is to build it, how many people the stadium needs to hold, how many hospitality suites for entertaining VIPs the team wants, and what other uses it might have besides hosting soccer games (such as music concerts or other sports events).

Even so, some rules of stadium design are universal. In theaters, cinemas, and stadiums, the farther back you go from the stage or screen or field, the higher the rows of seats get. They have to. Otherwise the back of the head of the person in front of you would be blocking the view.

In modern stadiums, the way the rows get higher follows a mathematical curve called a **parabola**. In this diagram of a cross section of a stand, you can see that farther from the field, the rows are higher. Funnily enough, when a ball is kicked through the air, it also follows a parabola, but one that is upside down and smaller.

You can't extend the parabola forever because most safety rules state that the angle between rows must be no greater than 34 degrees.

It's a good idea to have the front row of seats as close to the field as possible so the fans are close to the action. One trick to do this, which is used at Arsenal's Emirates Stadium, is to have spectators enter the stands from the top and then walk down, so there are no entrances taking up space at the bottom of the stands.

Another crucial part of the stadium is the roof. In hot countries, a roof is needed so fans are protected from the sun. In parts of the United States, fans need to be protected from the rain and snow.

In older stadiums, the roofs usually have support pillars to hold them up, but this is not ideal because the pillars obstruct some people's view. Thanks to advances in engineering science, however, it is now possible to design a roof that doesn't need support pillars in the stands—but you need to be very clever. "The most complicated part of stadium design is definitely the roof," a stadium engineer told us. "The roof of a stadium is like a bridge that is a fifth of a mile long. The pillars need to be well out of the way."

The requirement to have a roof that doesn't get in the way of spectators has led to some amazing, innovative stadium designs. At Wembley, for example, a gigantic arch 145 yards/133 meters high and 345 yards/315 meters wide helps support the roof. Wembley's arch is so big it can be seen all the way across London. In fact, it is twice as high as and 50 percent wider than London's Tower Bridge.

HOUSES OF FUN

Here is a whistle-stop tour of some of our favorite stadiums around the world.

STADIUM: De Kuip
TEAM: Feyenoord
COUNTRY: The Netherlands
BEST FOR: Good vibrations

Dear Soccer School students,
We just went to the bumpiest game ever! Our Dutch pal Wink took us to De Kuip. The stands are famous for vibrating when tens of thousands of fans jump up and down on them together, which happens after every Feyenoord goal. Wink has been coming here for years, and he told us that the first time he experienced it, he felt like he was in a rocket taking off! "It was amazing. And since then every time it has been fantastic," he said.

"The most accurate description is that you are in a boat and the river is wild." He says he finds it a bit scary even though he says it is perfectly safe. "It's being checked every season by engineers."
Chest bumps, Alex and Ben

STADIUM: A Pedreira
TEAM: Sporting de Braga
COUNTRY: Portugal
BEST FOR: Country views

Alex, meu amigo,
I'm watching a game played halfway up a mountain! Behind one of the goals is a sheer rock face that rises higher than the stadium—hence the name *pedreira*, which means "quarry" in Portuguese. I dig it! There are stands for 30,000 spectators on only two sides of the field, and behind the other goal is a dramatic

view across Braga and the surrounding countryside.
Kicks and hugs, Ben

1st

STADIUM: Allianz Arena
TEAM: Bayern Munich
COUNTRY: Germany
BEST FOR: Taking your pet chameleon

Lieber Ben!
This awesome stadium is enclosed in a shell made from diamond-shaped panels that light up in any color. For Bayern Munich games, the stadium is red, and for the German national team, it's white.

Shine on,
Alex

STADIUM: The Float at Marina Bay
TEAM: None
COUNTRY: Singapore
BEST FOR: Sea breezes

Dear Ben,
Bring your swim trunks out here! I'm at the Float, which is the world's largest floating stage. It's made entirely out of steel, and is located in Singapore's Marina Bay. You walk onto it along ramps from the mainland. There is a 30,000-seat stand on the mainland facing the stage, which gives a view of it from only one side. Turf was laid on the stage for a soccer game in 2008. So far that has been the only game played here! They hope more will happen in the future.
It floats my boat,
Alex

STADIUM: Borisov Arena
TEAM: BATE Borisov, Belarus national team
COUNTRY: Belarus
BEST FOR: Blowing bubbles

Dear Alex,
Are you dotty for stadiums? Then you will love the Borisov Arena! Its silvery shell is full of large, blob-shaped holes, which makes it look like massive bubbles are rising from the ground. It could be the skeleton of a giant alien. It's spot-on!

See you around
(and around and around),
Ben

STADIUM: Timsah (or "Crocodile") Arena
TEAM: Bursaspor
COUNTRY: Turkey
BEST FOR: Snappy dressers

Dear Spike,
Check out this tail! We are in Bursa, Turkey's fourth biggest city, and the LOCAL team Bursaspor has a new stadium. The team is known as the Green Crocodiles, and they built the stadium in the shape of a giant green crocodile! A massive crocodile's head sticks out of the side of the stadium, making the stands look like

the croc's body and tail curled up.
Bitey-bye-bye!
Alex and Ben

ALEX BELLOS
NEAR WEMBLEY
LONDON
'TED KINGDOM

THEATER OF CHOCOLATE

Every stadium has its own character and personality. Here are some with the best nicknames:

STADIUM	TEAM	NICKNAME
Beijing National Stadium	2008 Olympic soccer final	The Bird's Nest
Estadio Alberto J. Armando	Boca Juniors (Argentina)	La Bombonera (The Chocolate Box)
Old Trafford	Manchester United (England)	The Theatre of Dreams
San Mamés	Athletic Bilbao (Spain)	La Catedral (The Cathedral)
Stade Geoffroy-Guichard	Saint-Étienne (France)	Le Chaudron (The Cauldron)

MIND GAMES

Some teams play naughty tricks in their home stadium to annoy the visiting team, in the hope that it will make their opponents play badly. We can't be sure which of these pranks have actually been used, since no team is going to fess up to such dastardly plans! But we've heard rumors of all of them (and, no, before you ask, we wouldn't let any of these happen at Soccer School).

⚽ Turning up the heat to maximum so the visitors feel uncomfortable

⚽ Turning off the water supply so they can't wash and prepare themselves properly

⚽ Painting the walls such a disgusting color combination that the players feel cold and ill

⚽ Putting pictures of home fans looking angry on all the walls, so the visitors feel scared

⚽ Polishing the floor so thoroughly that visiting players are at risk of slipping, making sure they have to tiptoe as they walk

⚽ Making the locker room as small as possible

⚽ Filling the room with obstacles, such as a table in the middle that means the visiting coach can't talk to all his team at once

← Trick distorting mirror

⚽ Hanging mirrors that are designed to make players look smaller than they are

SHARING IS CARING

Some teams would never dream of being so naughty. These teams all share their stadiums with their local rivals!

STADIUM	LOCATION	TEAM
Ajinomoto	Tokyo, Japan	Tokyo, Tokyo Verdy
Azadi	Tehran, Iran	Esteghlal, Persepolis
Maracanã	Rio de Janeiro, Brazil	Flamengo, Fluminense
San Siro	Milan, Italy	AC Milan, Inter Milan
Stadio Olimpico	Rome, Italy	Lazio, Roma
Teddy	Jerusalem, Israel	Beitar Jerusalem, Hapoel Jerusalem
Tele2 Arena	Stockholm, Sweden	Djurgårdens IF, Hammarby

STAR STUDENT

STAN SIRO

66 I need some support! 99

☆☆☆ STAR STUDENT Stats

Seating capacity in living room: 16
Birthday party attendance: 38
Preferred angle to read Soccer School books: 45°
Vibrates at: 300 Hz
Birthplace: Sheffield (the Steel City), England
Supports: Standard Liège (Belgium)
Fave player: Kemar Roofe
Trick: Towers over the opposition

ENGINEERING QUIZ

1. What do you do in a vomitory?

a) Vomit
b) Cough
c) Sneeze
d) Walk

2. The seats in a stadium are in the:

a) Lies
b) Kneels
c) Sits
d) Stands

3. What architectural feature was also Wombley's nickname before the old stadium was demolished and a new one built in its place?

a) The Gigantic Slide
b) The Twin Towers
c) The Pyramid Pitch
d) The Golden Arches

4. When building a stadium, safety rules say you must build one toilet per roughly how many people?

a) 10
b) 50
c) 100
d) 500

5. What is special about the Big Zero stadium in Macapá, Brazil?

a) It is incredibly small and used by ants.
b) Zero big teams call it their home ground.
c) The midfield line runs across the equator so each half is in a different hemisphere.
d) Alex opened the stadium with Pelé and kicked the first ever ball there.

Here's a simple tale:

THE BOYS WHO DREAMED BIG

Once upon a time, there were two schoolboys named Alex and Ben. The pals loved soccer, and they also loved reading. They devoured all kinds of books, and they grew up to become journalists, write Soccer School books, and live happily ever after. The end.

Here's another way to write the same story:

SOCCER TIMES

BEST BUDDIES WRITE BALL BOOK
Two soccer friends have come out with a book series about the beautiful game. The Soccer School series is written by Alex and Ben, two journalists who loved reading when they were kids.

The first version is written in the style of a fairy tale and the second in the style of a news report. Fairy tales often start with the words *Once upon a time*. They are written in a way that creates a sense of magic and wonder. The aim of a news report, however, is to tell the facts in as short and clear a way as possible. No magic allowed!

There are many other ways to tell stories, and we will see some of them in this lesson. But the writing style we will be looking at in greatest detail is **game reporting**. This is the style used to write about soccer games in newspapers and on websites.

Sharpen your pencils. We're ready to go!

REPORTING BACKWARD

A **game report** is an article that tells you the story of a soccer game. If you open the sports pages of a newspaper or look on a sports website, you will see many game reports.

The first rule of game reporting is that you start with the end. That might sound strange, but just think about it. What's the first thing you want to know about a game? What the coach had for breakfast? Who was in the line-ups? Whether it was raining when the teams kicked off? No—the first thing you want to know when you read a game report is who won! A game reporter will always write down the name of the winning team in the first sentence of the report.

This technique of starting with the end is very different from many other ways of telling stories. In a fairy tale, for example, you start at the beginning, and it is only at the end that you find out how things turn out. You don't start the story of "Little Red Riding Hood" by telling your reader that the Big Bad Wolf is killed.

But in the opening few lines of a game report, you must include a **summary**, or overview, of the main points of the game. This should include the winner, the final score, and the name of the goal scorers. It might also mention any other important incidents, such as a red card.

ONCE UPON A TIMES

LITTLE RED BEATS WOLF!

We're going to take you through how you would begin a report of the most famous games in soccer history. Can you see how all the important parts of the game have been summarized in the opening sentence? The report then continues by discussing key moments or talking points:

SOCCER ⚽ TIMES

ENGLAND WINS 1966 WORLD CUP

Geoff Hurst scored a dramatic hat trick as England beat West Germany 4–2 to win the World Cup for the first time.

Germany had evened the score at 2–2 with the last kick of the regular 90 minutes, but England went ahead in overtime thanks to a shot from Hurst, which rebounded off the crossbar and onto the goal line. It was ruled to have crossed the line before bouncing out.

As Germany looked to equalize, England captain Bobby Moore passed to Hurst, who scored a stunning final goal.

Game reports are written in the **third person**, which means that the players are referred to as *him, her,* or *them,* not as *me* or *you.* The choice of words must be kept simple, so the reports are easy to read. And they have many **verbs**, words that describe actions. Soccer games have a lot of action! *Scored, beat, evened,* and *crossed* are all verbs

Further into the report, you might mention less important moments in the game. You can include background information like the lineups, the weather, and, if it's relevant, maybe even what the coach had for breakfast! A report ends with a **conclusion**, a final few sentences that give an overall perspective on the game:

> As soon as the referee blew the final whistle, fans ran onto the field to salute their heroes. The greatest moment in the history of English soccer was complete.

By the end of the report, your reader should have a sense of what really happened in the game. A good game report will explain the game's key moments, its best players, and whether the result was fair.

TWO SIDES OF THE STORY

Let's take a moment to talk about fairness.

England fans were very happy when the referee judged that Geoff Hurst's controversial shot, which rebounded down after hitting the crossbar, had crossed the goal line before bouncing back into play. But what about the German fans? They were not so happy, as you can imagine!

Think about how a German game reporter might have written up the same game. Can you see how this report is different from the one we just looked at?

FUSSBALL ⚽ ZEITUNG

WEST GERMANY ROBBED OF 1966 WORLD CUP

West Germany was unlucky to lose a controversial game 4–2 after one of England's goals was allowed even though the ball did not fully cross the line.

Just like the first game report, the important information, such as who won the game and the final score, is in the opening sentence. But this time the focus is on West Germany losing the game rather than on England winning. For the Germans, the key incident of the game was the controversial goal, not the hat trick by Geoff Hurst.

The rest of a German game report might go like this:

West Germany had taken an early lead when Helmut Haller scored after 12 minutes, but they needed Wolfgang Weber to equalize with the last kick of the regular 90 minutes.

Swiss referee Gottfried Dienst's decision in overtime that Hurst's shot had bounced over the goal line after hitting the crossbar was costly for West Germany. It was controversial since Dienst could not see the incident and couldn't speak the same language as the linesman from Azerbaijan. The West German team feels that the referee helped England win the game. Without a doubt, Hurst's goal will be debated for decades.

The English and the German reports make for very different reading, even though they are both talking about the same game.

This is because the game reporters made different decisions about what they thought was important in the game. They did so because they were writing for different audiences.

Soccer is full of incidents that divide opinion like this. This is what makes it fun to watch—and it also keeps game reporters on their toes!

A DAY IN THE LIFE OF A GAME REPORTER

A game reporter has to send in a report as soon as the final whistle blows so that people can read the story online the moment the game finishes. How do you write a story so quickly? Ben used to write game reports, so he can explain the tricks of the trade.

BEN'S GAME-DAY DIARY

1:00 My editor tells me how many words I need to write—it could be up to 1,000 words.

2:00 I arrive at the stadium and pick up my ticket.

2:15 I eat. All professional teams provide meals for the press.

2:45 I go to the press box, the section of the stands reserved for journalists. It has the best view: usually near the midfield line so you can see both goals. The seats have desks and little TVs that show replays.

3:00 The game begins! I watch about 30 minutes before I start typing. I describe any goals or exciting incidents. It's hard to type and follow the game, but the crowd noise is a good indicator of when to pay attention.

3:45 By halftime I have written about 400 words. I e-mail what I've written, which is called a runner, to my editor, who checks it for spelling mistakes and thinks of a headline.

4:30 I continue writing up the best parts and start to think about the beginning and the ending—the top and the tail—of the story. Seventy-five minutes into the game, I send what I've done to my editor. With 15 minutes to go, the story is pretty much written. Once I've sent the top and the tail, I cross my fingers that there are no more goals. Fans love it when their team scores a winning goal in the final minutes, but it's stressful for me as I'll have to rewrite the top and tail—and only have a few minutes to do it. In fact, the noise of journalists frantically typing is almost as loud as the fans' cheers!

4:45 I finish writing on the final whistle. My story is published online. But I can't go home yet.

5:00 The team coaches go into a room one at a time to answer questions from journalists.

5:30 I quickly rewrite the story to include anything interesting that the coaches said—and add any extra details I forgot the first time! This is the second version of the story.

5:45 When the players leave the locker rooms for the team bus, they walk through the "mixed zone," a room full of journalists. The players can choose to talk to reporters if they want to. Mixed zones can be very busy. You need good hearing, sturdy legs, and sharp elbows to survive! Usually, the comments from players will be used in a separate story the following day.
By this time I'm exhausted, and it's time to go home.

WRITING WITH STYLE

A game report is the correct writing style for a newspaper or a sports website. As we saw earlier, game reports are in the third person, with simple language and many verbs.

But there are other writing styles, such as **poetry**, **narrative**, or **dialogue**, which have their own techniques for telling stories. They may not give you as much detail as a game report, but they can bring out other elements of what happened. Which one do you prefer?

AND VERILY, most Mightily did Sir Geoffrey Smite the Leathery globe into the Onion Bag for the glory of this sceptred Isle.

LIMERICK

Style summary: a funny rhyming poem, five lines long.

> There once was a striker called Hurst,
> Whose World Cup hat trick was a first.
> Each time that he scored,
> The Wembley fans roared.
> West Germany left feeling cursed.

HAIKU

Style summary: a poem of seventeen beats, or syllables, in three lines of five, seven, and five syllables, respectively.

> England are world champs
> Beat West Germany 4–2
> Arise, Sir Geoff Hurst

DIARY

Style summary: first person, meaning told from the perspective of one individual who shares their opinions and emotions.

Dear Diary,

My name is Geoffrey, and I am twenty-four years old. Yesterday I played for England in the World Cup final and scored three goals! We won 4-2 and the whole country celebrated. My mom told me I might be knighted. That would be so exciting! What I really want is to win the League with my team, West Ham, and win the World Cup again one day. I wonder if that might happen. If not, I hope I will be remembered in a book series called Soccer School!

DIALOGUE

Style summary: a conversation that tells its own story.

GEOFFREY: Thanks for that pass, Bobby. It set me up perfectly to score my third goal!

BOBBY: You played so well, young Geoffrey. I'm so happy we won the World Cup!

GEOFFREY: It's a dream come true. And you, our fantastic England captain, will soon be lifting the World Cup trophy!

PHONE ME IN

Before computers and e-mails, journalists used to read their game reports over the phone to typists in the office. Sometimes a crackly line could lead to embarrassing mistakes. In 1998, one reporter called his newspaper to say that England fans were involved in a fight in France during the World Cup. He ended by saying: "A police van drew up containing a dozen armed gendarmes." A gendarme is a French policeman. The typist on the other end of the line misheard, and in the next day's paper, it was reported that the police turned up with "a dozen armed John Barnes"—the former Liverpool winger who had recently played for England. But there is only one of him! *Mon dieu!*

SAMMY COLON

☆ STAR STUDENT

66 Get it down! 99

☆☆☆ STAR STUDENT **Stats**

Typing speed: 120 words per minute

Syl-la-bles in his name: 4

Biggest headline font: 28 pt

Daily stories read before breakfast: 14

Birthplace: Story City, Iowa

Supports: Reading (U.K.)

Fave Player: Christen Press

Trick: Reads the game brilliantly

☆

ENGLISH QUIZ

1. **When a reporter sends through their final game report, what have they added at the last minute?**

a) Top and tail
b) Heads and tails
c) Fairy tale
d) Gareth Bale

2. **"Some people are on the pitch! They think it's all over!" What were the next words that BBC commentator Kenneth Wolstenholme used to describe England's fourth goal in the 1966 World Cup final?**

a) "Get off the pitch!"
b) "Come on, England!"
c) "It is now!"
d) "Oh, Mr. Hurst, I think I love you!"

3. **The U.K.'s first newspaper was published in November 1665. What was it called?**

a) *The Times of London*
b) *The Oxford Gazette*
c) *The Newcastle Argus*
d) *Your News Week*

4. **How did the names of former Wales strikers Ian Rush and Mark Hughes supposedly once appear in a game report that was phoned in over a crackly line?**

a) Russian Jews
b) Rushing Poos
c) Rushing Whos
d) Russian News

5. **Which team won the 1999 Champions League final by beating Bayern Munich 2–1 after scoring two goals in the last three minutes of injury-time—forcing journalists to rewrite their game reports in double-quick time?**

a) Chelsea
b) Arsenal
c) Manchester United
d) Liverpool

RELIGIOUS STUDIES

What does soccer teach us?

We know that to be a top athlete, you have to practice, exercise, and eat well; we learn complicated regulations like the offside rule; we discover weird facts such as English team Everton's nickname being the Toffees.

But there are other things we learn from soccer too. Things that have nothing to do with soccer, but are instead about how we live our lives. Is that deep or what?

Traditionally people have looked to religion for guidance about how to live their lives. There are many religions in the world, and they all have similar messages about how to be a good person, such as stating you should not kill or steal.

Today we are going to see how some of the life lessons that religion teaches us can also be found in soccer.

Hallelujah!

FAITH ROVERS

A religion is a system of beliefs about the meaning of life.
Not everyone belongs to a religion, and that's fine too!
Here are five of the world's major religions and how
they compare.

RELIGION	WHEN FOUNDED	HOW MANY FOLLOWERS	KEY FIGURES
Buddhism	More than 2,500 years ago	Around 0.5 billion	Buddha
Christianity	2,000 years ago	Around 2.2 billion	God, Jesus Christ
Hinduism	More than 3,000 years ago	Around 1 billion	Brahma, Shiva, Vishnu
Islam	1,400 years ago	Around 1.7 billion	Allah, Muhammad
Judaism	More than 3,000 years ago	Around 17 million	God, Abraham, Moses

CENTRAL BELIEFS	PLACE OF WORSHIP	SPECIAL OBSERVANCES
The way to free oneself from suffering— and achieve a state called nirvana—is to follow the teachings of Buddha. Followers learn how to meditate, which is a way to empty the mind of thoughts.	Temple	Vesak, which celebrates Buddha's birthday
God sent his son, Jesus Christ, to Earth in order to save humankind from the consequences of its own bad behavior. Jesus was killed on the cross, but came to life again three days later.	Church	Christmas, which celebrates the birth of Jesus Christ
The soul is eternal, and after death it may be born again, or reincarnated, into a different body, such as an animal or a plant. The sacred Hindu texts are called the Vedas.	Temple	Diwali, or the Festival of Lights, celebrates the symbolic victory of light over dark
Allah sent his prophet Muhammad to Earth. Through Muhammad, Allah's words were written in the Qur'an, Islam's holy book.	Mosque	Ramadan, which commemorates the revelation of the Qur'an to Muhammad
God formed a covenant with the Israelites, and later gave them the Torah, their holy book, through the prophet Moses.	Synagogue	Yom Kippur, the day when Jews fast and ask for forgiveness

LIFE LESSON 1:
IT FEELS GOOD TO BELONG

Most human beings love to feel like part of something. It is comforting to know that there are other people in the world like us, who share our beliefs and our passions. Traditionally, we get this sense of community from our family, our friends, and our religion. Most religions have rituals and festivals that bring people together, like Christmas for Christians and Ramadan for Muslims.

In western Europe, where people are less religious than they used to be, many people now get a sense of belonging in other ways, such as by supporting a soccer team. When we meet someone who supports the same team as us, we immediately feel a connection with them. When we are in a soccer stadium surrounded by thousands of fans of the same team, this sense of belonging can be amazing—especially when we are all singing the same song!

TEAM	"PLACE OF WORSHIP"	FAVORITE "HYMN"
Bayern Munich	Allianz Arena	"Stern des Südens"
Juventus	Juventus Stadium	"Storia di Un Grande Amore"
Manchester United	Old Trafford	"Glory, Glory, Man United"
Marseille	Vélodrome	"Allez l'OM!"
Real Madrid	Santiago Bernabéu	"Hala Madrid y Nada Más!"

LIFE LESSON 2:
HAVE A SENSE OF SOMETHING LARGER THAN YOU

Every religion has a belief system that allows its followers to think about their role and position in the universe. It provides us with answers to big questions, such as where have we come from and what happens when we die. Religions, in other words, give us a sense of being part of something much bigger than ourselves, which many people find comforting.

What is a soccer team? For sure, it is bigger than any single person or thing. A team is made up of the players, the stadium, the fans, the songs, the trophies, the uniforms, the games, and much else besides. Fans' deep love for their team is a way of being devoted to something larger than they are—something that has existed for decades before they were born, and will continue to exist after they die.

I'M DYING TO SEE THEM WIN

Some fans are so devoted to their team that they want to be with them even after they die. Several teams have opened cemeteries for supporters, where gravestones are adorned with team scarves and choirs sing team anthems. Here are some teams that you can support from beyond the grave:

Boca Juniors (Argentina): Boca's field was damaged when families of fans scattered ashes of loved ones on it, so now Boca has its own burial site. It has reserved a plot for its most famous player, Diego Maradona.

Corinthians (Brazil): There is room for the remains of seventy thousand fans at the Corinthians Forever cemetery. The team says the cemetery is "for those who are fans from the beginning to the end."

Schalke 04 (Germany): The team offers baptism and wedding services, and now has a cemetery for fans. No wonder their team song contains the line "a lifelong blue-and-white."

LIFE LESSON 3:
LOSING IS AS IMPORTANT AS WINNING

Religions bring people together for happy celebrations. But religions also have rituals where followers must experience some form of suffering. For example, followers of certain religions must deprive themselves of something during particular religious festivals or holy days. Christians give up habits, such as eating chocolate, during Lent. Jews, Muslims, Hindus, and Buddhists all observe periods of **fasting**, which means they stop eating altogether. The idea behind these rituals is that in order to appreciate how comfortable your life is, you must experience what it is like to be without that comfort. You need to experience suffering to fully experience joy. The message is that sometimes we win and sometimes we lose. Both winning and losing are inevitable facts of life.

We all like it when our team wins, but being a soccer fan is not just about winning. It is also about losing. All soccer fans know the gut-wrenching, tear-inducing feeling of disappointment when their team loses an important game. Winning and losing are equal parts of the game.

Fans learn to savor the victories. But we also learn how to cope with the defeats. There are good things about losing, even though it might not seem so at the time! Losing often brings out the best in your friendships, as you comfort each other in defeat. It makes you realize that life has ups and downs. The bad times are what make the good times such happy ones.

GOD SQUAD

These soccer players went on to do religious work:
Peter Knowles (Wolverhampton Wanderers)
Phil Mulryne (Manchester United, Norwich, Northern Ireland)
Gavin Peacock (Newcastle, Chelsea, Queens Park Rangers)
Carlos Roa (Racing, RCD Mallorca, Argentina)
Taribo West (Inter Milan, Derby Town, Nigeria)

LIFE LESSON 4:
NEVER GIVE UP HOPE

Religion gives people hope when things get really bad. Many religions encourage prayer, through which you can ask God for help. (Yes, you can ask God to look kindly on your soccer team too, but there is no proof that it works!) Some religions also offer hope to believers by saying that when we die, our souls will go to Heaven, a happy place. Others teach us that life is constantly changing and that we can always change it for the better.

At Soccer School, we think that whatever religion you believe in—or even if you don't have a religion—you should never give up on your hopes and

PENALTY SHOOT-OUT

dreams. And as a soccer fan, you never give up hope, since there are many times when teams have triumphed against the odds. Our favorite example is the 2005 Champions League final between Liverpool and AC Milan.

THE MIRACLE OF ISTANBUL

The halftime score was AC Milan 3, Liverpool 0. The thousands of fans who had traveled from England to watch the game in Istanbul, Turkey, were looking at a humiliating defeat.

A few Liverpool fans left before the second half, but the majority stayed and sang a rousing rendition of the Liverpool anthem, "You'll Never Walk Alone." Inside the locker room, the players could hear the song. It lifted their spirits. The coach, Rafael Benitez, changed the tactics for the second half. It worked: in the space of six minutes in that second half, Liverpool scored three goals. Suddenly it was 3–3. The fans kept singing for their team!

The game went to a penalty shoot-out, and Jerzy Dudek was the hero; he kept out three penalties, and Liverpool won the game!

The moral of Liverpool's amazing triumph is that no matter how bad things are, the good days may be just around the corner. In Liverpool's case, it took only six minutes to turn around what seemed like an impossible situation.

AGAINST ALL ODDS

Here are some more soccer miracles:

Nottingham Forest
Title: European Cup 1979, 1980
Just after their promotion to the top flight in 1978, Forest went on to win the next two European Cups, in 1979 and 1980.

Hellas Verona
Title: Serie A 1984–1985
The little team only lost two games all season and stunned Italy's big teams by winning the only title in the team's history.

Denmark
Title: Euro 1992
Denmark hadn't even qualified for the tournament but was recalled from their vacation after Yugoslavia was banned. Denmark then beat Germany in the final.

Greece
Title: Euro 2004
No one thought defensive-minded Greece stood a chance, but they beat Czech Republic in the semifinal and Portugal, the favorites and hosts, in the final.

Leicester City
Title: 2015–2016 Premier League
Leicester had only just avoided relegation to a lower league the previous season, but they stunned the richer teams around them by winning the title in dramatic style.

CHURCH OF MARADONA

One of the best soccer players in history even has a religion named after him. The Church of Maradona is an organization that worships Diego Maradona. It celebrates two important days in the life of Argentina's most famous player: October 30, Diego's birthday, and June 22, the date of his two goals against England in the 1986 World Cup quarterfinal. The church has over eighty thousand members, and Maradona fans have even gotten married at his altar. "It's logical," says one of the church's founders, Hernán Amez. "Soccer is a religion to Argentinians; every religion has its god, and the god of soccer is Diego."

CHRISTIAN TEMPLE

★ STAR STUDENT

66 Have faith! 99

★★★ STAR STUDENT **Stats**

Prayers before bedtime: 12
Beliefs about soccer: 21,233
Fasting days per year: 3
Farting days per year: 362
Birthplace: Hornchurch, England
Supports: Washington Spirit (United States)
Fave player: Allan Saint-Maximin
Trick: Always present everywhere on the field

RELIGIOUS STUDIES QUIZ

1. Which is the world's biggest religion?

a) Christianity
b) Hinduism
c) Islam
d) Jedi

2. Which Premier League team had two players named Jesus in the 2016–2017 season?

a) Manchester City
b) Liverpool
c) Southampton
d) Chelsea

3. What is the traditional Buddhist position for meditating?

a) Curled up in bed
b) Sitting down
c) Standing on one foot
d) Hanging from a tree

4. What is English team Liverpool's 2005 Champions League final win over AC Milan known as?

a) The Wonder of Gerrard
b) The Revelation of Dudek
c) The Marvel of Benitez
d) The Miracle of Istanbul

5. Argentine goalkeeper Carlos Roa refused to do what for religious reasons when he played for Spanish team RCD Mallorca?

a) Make any saves
b) Cut his hair
c) Play soccer before sunset on Saturdays
d) Go to church with his teammates

BALANCE
AFTER-SCHOOL CLUB

DON'T SKIP THIS

Soccer players need to be fit, fast, agile, and have a great sense of balance. In this after-school club, we will look at one of the best ways to practice these things at the same time, which is ... jumping rope. You thought jumping rope was easy? Think again. Boxers are well known for incorporating jumping rope into their training routines, and soccer players do it now too. It's a great workout without putting too much stress on your joints. Hop to it!

Jump 1: Double jump

Jump as high as you can and swing the rope fast, so you get the rope under your feet twice while you are in the air.

GOOD FOR: Increasing pulse rate
DIFFICULTY RATING: 1/4

Jump 2: Run jumps

You need some space, as this involves jogging and jumping rope without stopping your running motion.

GOOD FOR: Improving fitness and balance
DIFFICULTY RATING: 2/4

Feeling ropy!

Jump 3: High Knees

Instead of lifting both feet off the ground at the same time and at the same height, run in place and jump; then raise one knee at a time. It's tiring, so only try it for a few swings before going back to normal jumping.

GOOD FOR: Building leg strength
DIFFICULTY RATING: 3/4

Jump 4: Crossover

Lift both feet while jumping and swinging the rope normally. Then quickly cross your arms in front of you, stretching your hands as far apart as they can go, and jump through the loop you create. Then cross your hands back so you are jumping normally. It might take some practice to get the loop size right, but it will happen!

GOOD FOR: Pushing off strongly in sprints
DIFFICULTY RATING: 4/4

BEAT IT

The number of times your heart beats every minute is your pulse. When you're jumping rope, your pulse should be about 130 beats per minute. To find your pulse, touch the side of your neck until you feel the regular beat. Count how many beats you feel in 10 seconds. Multiply this number by 6 and you have the number of beats per minute.

Hands up if you know what **handedness** is! Handedness is the curious way that some people use a pen, ring a doorbell, or pick their nose with their right hand, while other people prefer their left hand. Nearly all of us use one hand to do most tasks. If we prefer to use the right hand, we are right-handed, and if we prefer the left, we are left-handed.

We do the same thing with other parts of the body too, such as our eyes and our ears. You might always use your left eye to peer through a keyhole. Or you might always hold your phone to your right ear when you answer it. This is known as **eyedness** and **earedness**.

Let's carry on down to our feet. Most of us prefer to kick a ball with either our left or our right foot. In this lesson we're going to look at **footedness** in soccer. Are there any advantages to being right-footed or left-footed either on or off the field? We're going to investigate the rivalry behind our left and right sides.

Come on; let's get this lesson off on the right foot! Don't get left behind!

ALL RIGHTY

First things first: Why is there such a thing as handedness, anyway? Some scientists say it is because training one hand for a task makes you more skillful at it than if you divided the work between both hands. Being as skillful as possible was very important for survival when we lived in the wild hundreds of thousands of years ago.

For example, imagine two cavemen learning to throw stones. And imagine that one of the cavemen only used his right hand, but the other used his right hand half the time and his left hand the other half the time. The one using only his right hand would end up having the better throw, since his right hand would be getting much more practice than either of the hands of the caveman who used both. And if he had the best throw, he would find it easier to throw stones to kill animals for food.

You've probably noticed among your friends that right-handedness is more common. Both Alex and Ben are right-handed.

In fact, so are nine out of every ten people in the world. One amazing aspect of handedness is that it begins from before you are even born. One study found that nine out of ten babies who suck their thumb in the womb do so with their right hand — the same proportion who end up becoming right-handed as adults.

Professor Chris McManus at University College London is a world expert on handedness. He thinks that originally all humans were right-handed. He doesn't know why left-handedness developed, or why there are so many more right-handed people than there are left-handed people. What scientists do know is that half a million years ago, there were already some left-handers. They figured this out by looking at fossilized teeth samples. Many of the teeth had scratches at one angle from cutting animal skin while holding it in the right hand, but some teeth had scratches at another angle from cutting animal skin while holding it in the left hand. Chew, gross!

LEFT ISN'T RIGHT

Throughout history there have always been fewer lefties than righties, and in many different cultures it seems that lefties have had a worse deal. In ancient Rome, public speakers wore togas that restricted their left sides, which meant lefties couldn't make gestures with their good hand. In Europe in the Middle Ages, left-handedness was associated with the devil and witchcraft.

The bad rep for lefties has continued into the modern era. In India, many people eat with their hands, but only the right hand. It is seen as rude to eat with the left hand, because that hand is used for wiping your butt! In Ghana, in Africa, pointing with your left hand is frowned upon.

In many languages, the word *right* is associated with good things and the word *left* with bad. In English, *right* means correct. Compare that with the meanings of the word *left* in these languages:

LANGUAGE	WORD FOR LEFT	OTHER MEANING
French	Gauche	Awkward
German	Links/Link	Underhanded
Italian	Sinistra/Sinistro	Sinister
Danish	Kejte	Clumsy
Polish	Lewy	Shady
Portuguese	Canhoto	Devil
Turkish	Sol	Odd

LET'S SHAKE ON THAT

Even in soccer, players are encouraged to use their right hands. Before every Premier League game and Major League Soccer game, players shake hands as a gesture of respect. But why do they use their right hands to do this? Some historians think the reason dates back to ancient Greek times, when everyone carried a weapon. If you met someone new, putting out your right hand to show you weren't holding a weapon was a sign of friendship. The up-and-down motion of the handshake was meant to dislodge any knives that might be hidden up a sleeve.

LEFT BEHIND?

Being left-handed isn't always easy, because many things are designed for people who are right-handed. Here are everyday objects that lefties often struggle with:

OBJECT	REASON
Camera	Need to use weaker right finger to press shutter
Pen	Left hand smudges the ink as it moves across the page
Pencil sharpener	Difficult to twist a pencil clockwise with your left hand
Scissors	Hard to grip right-handed scissors and cut cleanly
Zipper	Need to use weaker right hand to pull zipper

But being left-handed has its advantages too. Surveys have shown that left-handers spend less time in store lines. This is because people have a tendency to choose the checkout line on their dominant side. So since there are more righties than lefties, lines on the right tend to be busier than lines on the left.

Professor McManus believes that left-handers' brains are wired in a different way from right-handers', which can sometimes make them more creative people, excelling in music and poetry. Five of the last eight American presidents have been left-handed — many more than you would expect. The same is true of the winners of Nobel Prizes.

However, Professor McManus warns that it can work the other way. This same brain wiring causes some left-handers to have problems with aspects of speech and language.

LIFE IS SO ONE-SIDED

As you now know, nine out of ten people are right-handed. As a percentage this means that 90 percent of people are right-handed and 10 percent are left-handed. The approximate percentages for right dominance and left dominance are different for the other parts of the body:

BODY PART	RIGHTIES	LEFTIES
Hand	90%	10%
Foot	80%	20%
Eye	70%	30%
Ear	60%	40%

LEFT FOOT FORWARD

If you are right-footed, it is more natural to play in a position on the right side of the field. This is because your dominant right leg will be closer to the touchline, meaning you are able to use the full width of the field. Likewise, if you are left-footed, it is more natural to play on the left.

You might have thought that the tendency for righties to be on the right and lefties to be on the left means that you would want more or less the same number of lefties and righties on a team. Surprisingly, however, this is not the case. Dr. David Carey of Bangor University found that approximately 80 percent of professional soccer players are right-footed and 20 percent left-footed, which is the same percentage for the population as a whole. Dr. Carey based his figures on some games from two World Cups and one full Premier League season. The fact that the majority of players on any team are right-footed means that often right-footers play on the left. When they play on their "wrong" side, they need to adjust their body shape in order to make the most of that position.

Left is best!

Some of soccer's best-ever players were left-footed. Here are our five greatest players of all time (but not in order). Four are left-footed!

FIVE GREATEST PLAYERS

Johan Cruyff (The Netherlands): Lefty
Diego Maradona (Argentina): Lefty
Lionel Messi (Argentina): Lefty
Pelé (Brazil): Righty
Ferenc Puskás (Hungary): Lefty

Our list is a small sample size, but that number is way higher than the 20 percent average in soccer. Maybe it's because right-footers find it harder to play against left-footers because they are rarer—or that lefties are more successful because they are used to finding solutions in a right-handed world!

In some sports, being left-handed can definitely be an advantage. The percentage of successful left-handed professionals in cricket, tennis, baseball, fencing, and boxing—where left-handers are known as "southpaws"—is also much higher than average. Experts think it's because being left-handed adds an element of surprise to their game, as right-handers have less experience playing against lefties.

Hey, am-bipedal!

So am I!

EQUAL FOOTING

Dr. Carey's research also showed that players use their dominant foot 80 percent of the time on the field—but that they are actually more successful with their passes when using their other, weaker foot. He thinks that this is because players tend to use their weaker foot in easy situations and make risky passes with the dominant foot.

Some people can be equally good with both their left and right sides. Those who are equally good with their right and left hands are called **ambidextrous**, from the Latin *ambi*, meaning "both," and *dexter* meaning "right side."

The foot equivalent of ambidextrous is **ambipedal**, although if a soccer player is just as good with either foot we say they are **two-footed**—even though all professional players have two feet! Dr. Carey calculated that only one in one thousand male players is truly two-footed.

Spanish midfielder Santi Cazorla is two-footed. He once injured his right foot (his dominant one at the time) and then practiced with his left so much that now he can take corner kicks with either foot—and he doesn't even know which is better! And it turns out that Cazorla was onto something: another study of over three thousand players showed that left-footed players earn a little more money than their right-footed colleagues. But those who are two-footed can earn up to 15 percent more than right-footed players.

TOP TWO-FOOTED PLAYERS
Santi Cazorla (Spain)
Ousmane Dembélé (France)
Tobin Heath (USA)
Paolo Maldini (Italy)
Christian Pulisic (USA)
Alex Morgan (USA)

RIGHT GIRLS

We said that 90 percent of the population is right-handed and 10 percent is left-handed. If we separate those numbers into men and women, we see that 12 percent of men are lefties, but only 9 percent of women are. No one knows why more men are left-handed, but it could be because girls born left-handed are more likely to switch handedness.

This also applies on the field. Dr. Carey looked at all the women who played in the 2011 World Cup finals and the 2012

Boys 12%.
Girls 9%.
Left-handedness

Olympics. He compared this to his data on male players and discovered that women players are on average less likely to be left-footed and more likely to be two-footed.

FOOT	SOCCER PLAYERS (FEMALE)	SOCCER PLAYERS (MALE)
Right-footed	87.5%	79.8%
Left-footed	11.1%	20.1%
Two-footed	1.3%	0.1%

CROSSED PLAYERS

Some players have their handedness and footedness all mixed up! These soccer players are right-handed but left-footed:

Patrice Evra (France)
Hugo Lloris (France)
Lionel Messi (Argentina)
Danny Rose (England)
David Silva (Spain)

SAM B. DEXTROUS

☆ STAR STUDENT

66 Left! Right! Left! Right! 99

☆☆☆ STAR STUDENT | Stats

Dominance of right hand: 60%.
Dominance of left ear: 30%.
Dominance of right nostril: 80%.
Dominance of left buttock: 75%.
Birthplace: Left Bank, Paris
Supports: Brighton (U.K.)
Fave player: Heather Mitts
Trick: Great with both feet

BIOLOGY QUIZ

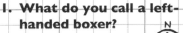

1. What do you call a left-handed boxer?

a) Northpaw
b) Eastpaw
c) Westpaw
d) Southpaw

2. In what sport is it illegal to play left-handed?

a) Golf
b) Polo
c) Badminton
d) Tiddlywinks

3. Which animal is almost exclusively left-handed?

a) Meerkat
b) Frog
c) Kangaroo
d) Baboon

4. Paolo Maldini played over nine hundred games for AC Milan and won seven Italian league titles and five Champions League titles with them. He was two-footed. Which of the following is true?

a) One of his feet was two sizes bigger than the other.
b) He spent his whole career playing as a left-back.
c) He was scared to shoot with his right foot.
d) The only goals he ever scored were with his head.

5. What are the chances of one identical twin being left-handed and the other right-handed?

a) 0 percent
b) 20 percent
c) 50 percent
d) 100 percent

Soccer is about numbers. It's a game of eleven versus eleven, for ninety minutes, in which each team tries to score a greater number of goals than its opponent. League standings are grids of digits: wins, draws, losses, games played, goal difference, and total points. All these numbers are why Alex loves it!

But that's just the beginning. Soccer is full of **data** and **statistics (or stats)**, which are facts that can be described with numbers. Before a game, you will hear commentators give team stats, such as how many times the teams have played each other before and which team won the most times. After a game, there will be data to show how long each team had possession of the ball, how many shots on goal there were, and many other facts. A data deluge! A swamp of statistics!

In this lesson, we are going to find out how soccer data is collected and then look at how it can be used to give us fascinating insights into the game.

Let the countdown begin!

SPEED DATA

At the beginning of every English Premier League game, in an office far away from the stadium, two people sit in front of a bank of computer screens, ready to turn that game into numbers.

As soon as the whistle is blown, these **data gatherers** start typing away on their keyboards. *Tap, tap, tap, tap!* The moment a player touches the ball, they type in his shirt number and also what he does with the ball, such as *pass* or *cross*, from a list of many actions. There are two data gatherers because getting all that information is too much for just one person to do. They split the load — one types in the data for the home team and the other for the away team.

The data gatherers must stay focused for the entire game so that every detail is captured. No sneezing or scratching your butt! As well as *pass* and *cross*, there are about fifty different events they need to type in if they see them happening on the field. Some are obvious and easy to register, such as *goal*, *corner*, and *red card*. But there are others that require eagle eyes and good judgment, such as *flick on, good skill*, and *interception*. One of the screens has an aerial diagram of the field, on which they click the position of the ball each time it is kicked.

At the end of the game, the gatherers quickly check for mistakes, and then send all the data to companies like TV networks and newspapers. Then they can finally relax. It's been an exhausting ninety minutes for their eyes, fingers, and brains.

GATHERING GIFTS

Gathering soccer data is done by humans rather than by computer since computers are not good enough (yet!) to do the job well. For example, when a dozen players jump together for a ball from a corner, a human data gatherer is able to judge who headed the ball by looking at details like the players' facial expressions, hairstyles, and maybe even the color of their shoes. Computers don't have a clue!

Most tackles in a season . . .

Most corner kicks . . .

Fewest injuries . . .

Most miles run in 90 minutes . . .

Most passes in a game . . .

Most crosses . . .

Most saves . . .

Being a data gatherer sounds like a fun job, since all you do is watch soccer games. But not every human has the required skills. You need to have very good **hand-eye coordination**, which means that you can move your hands based on what you see very quickly and accurately. Gatherers know exactly where to move their hands on the keyboard without ever looking down.

Most people who apply to be gatherers don't have the necessary technical skills to do the job. Those who do must first spend four to six weeks training on demo games for eight hours a day. After the training, it still takes several months to become confident. During any one game, the gatherers will register about two thousand pieces of data, which works out as one piece of data about every two seconds. That's what you call being on the ball!

Highest number of red cards . . .

STATS R US

We collect all this data in order to understand the game better. Numbers allow us to discover soccer facts that we would not otherwise know. If we look at data from the history of English soccer's top flight (meaning the First Division from 1888–1992, and the Premier League from 1992–2017), then it is easy to find out some very intriguing stats.

NUMBERS GAME

7 goals were scored by Ted Drake for Arsenal against Aston Villa in December 1935, which remains the most goals ever scored by a player in a single game in the top league of English football.

0-0 is the most common score in the Premier League.

89 minutes is the most likely minute of the game in regular time for a goal to be scored (excluding goals scored at **45** minutes and **90** minutes, because these take into account injury time).

168 passes were made by Yaya Touré when playing for Manchester City against Stoke City in December 2011: the most passes any Premier League player has made since this data was first gathered in **2006**.

And that's Ted's seventh!

PERFECT PERCENTAGES

Sometimes we need to do some math to make the statistics easier to understand. Today we're going to learn about **percentages** and **averages**.

Percentages are a way to describe amounts as a proportion of one hundred, and are used as a way to make different numbers easy to compare. For example, this diagram shows the areas of the field from which all goals were scored in the Premier League, 1992–2017:

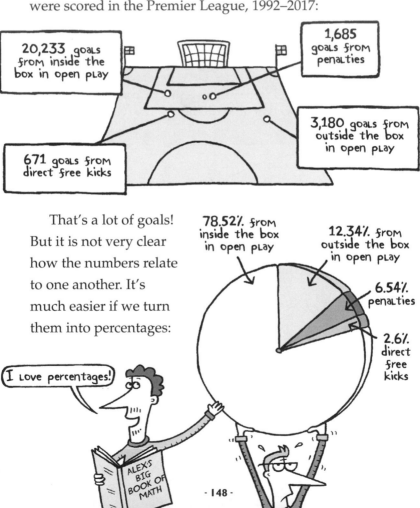

20,233 goals from inside the box in open play

1,685 goals from penalties

3,180 goals from outside the box in open play

671 goals from direct free kicks

That's a lot of goals! But it is not very clear how the numbers relate to one another. It's much easier if we turn them into percentages:

78.52% from inside the box in open play

12.34% from outside the box in open play

6.54% penalties

2.6% direct free kicks

I love percentages!

ALEX'S BIG BOOK OF MATH

The numbers in the pie chart mean that out of every one hundred goals, about seventy-nine came from inside the box in open play, about twelve came from outside the box in open play, about seven came from penalties, and about three came from direct free kicks (rounding to the nearest number). One hundred is a nice easy number to make comparisons from, which is why percentages make things easier to understand.

PERCENTAGE PROBLEM

Since Ben loves penalties, we'll show him here how to calculate the percentage of goals scored by penalties. First, we need to count the total number of goals of all kinds, which adds up to 25,769. Then we divide the number of goals scored from penalties by the total, like this:

$1,685 \div 25,769 = 0.0654$

Then we multiply this by 100:

$0.0654 \times 100 = 6.54\%$

There we have it! 6.54% of goals are scored from penalties. The way of calculating percentages is always the same: divide the number of particular events (e.g., how a goal is scored) by the number of total events (e.g., all goals scored) and then multiply by 100.

Sometimes soccer coaches say that their team "gave 110 percent," which means that soccer coaches are very bad at math! No one can give more than 100 percent, since 100 percent of something means ALL of that thing. To say that the team gave 110 percent is an exaggeration that means the team gave everything they could give—and more. At Soccer School, we mock these coaches for not exaggerating enough. Here we insist on 111 percent!

AWESOME AVERAGES

Sometimes games have no goals (boo!) and sometimes games have lots of goals (yay!). We can use math to work out how many goals there are **on average** per game.

> The average number of goals per Premier League game is **2.64!**

This statistic does not mean that in every match 2.64 goals are scored—that would be impossible! What it means is that sometimes there are fewer than 2.64 goals and sometimes there are more than 2.64 goals, but if we take all Premier League games from 1992–2017 together, then a good estimate for the typical number of goals is 2.64. This is the **average** number.

AVERAGE SUM

We calculate the average number of goals per game by adding up all the goals scored in all games and dividing them by the total number of games:

$25,769 \div 9,746 = 2.64$

The average number of goals per Premier League game between 2010 and 2017 is 2.75, a little bit higher than the average of all games between 1992 and 2017. Compare these figures to the averages in different leagues. In Germany you will see, on average, almost half a goal more per game than in France.

AUGUST 2010–2017	AVERAGE NUMBER OF GOALS PER GAME
German Bundesliga	2.90
Spanish La Liga	2.78
English Premier League	2.75
Italian Serie A	2.67
French Ligue 1	2.50

HOME RULES

Most soccer fans know that there is an advantage to playing at home, since teams tend to perform better in their own stadiums. There are many reasons why this is true, such as familiarity with the stadium, being surrounded by all your supporters, and not having to travel very far to get to the game. What's great about math is that we can use it to work out exactly how much better teams do at home than away.

HOME
Average number of goals per game scored by home teams: 1.53

AWAY
Average number of goals per game scored by away teams: 1.12

If teams score, on average, 1.53 goals per game at home but only 1.12 goals away, then, on average, teams are scoring 1.53 − 1.12 = 0.41 more goals when playing at home than when playing away. The home advantage is almost half a goal per game!

We score 0.41 more goals per game when we play at home!

ON TARGET

The shot conversion rate is the number of times a shot at goal will result in a goal. The percentage is calculated by dividing the number of shots that score goals by the number of all shots at goal. Here are the top ten best teams from 2010–2017. The average shot conversion rate across all teams is 12.91 percent, which shows how good the best ones are!

TEAM	SHOT CONVERSION RATE (%)
Barcelona	22.24
Real Madrid	19.38
RB Leipzig	19.08
Bayern Munich	18.52
Paris Saint-Germain	17.82
Manchester City	16.89
Manchester United	16.85
Monaco	16.69
Borussia Dortmund	16.62
Arsenal	16.38

BRIDGET DIGIT

STAR STUDENT

2 $x+y$ $+$
13 $\sqrt{7}$
5^2
8 $\div$
$\times$

66 I'm not average! 99

STAR STUDENT Stats

Favorite band: One Direction
Favorite book: Catch 22
Favorite candy bar: 100 Grand
Favorite equation: $7 \times 11 \times 13 = 1{,}001$
Birthplace: Ventimiglia, Italy
Supports: Twente (Netherlands)
Fave Player: Didier Six
Trick: Best in the division at division

MATH QUIZ

1. What is the word *stats* short for?

a) Statues
b) Statistics
c) Stalactites
d) Stationary

2. Which of these jobs requires the best hand-eye coordination?

a) Librarian
b) Teacher
c) Model
d) Bus driver

3. What is 50 percent of 90 minutes?

a) 45 minutes
b) 50 minutes
c) 90 minutes
d) 110 minutes

4. If a team plays four games and scores the following number of goals— 1, 1, 2, 4—in the games, what is the average number of goals the team scores per game?

a) 1
b) 2
c) 3
d) 4

5. What does the common phrase "big data" mean?

a) Data about tall people
b) A species of large dates grown in Cyprus
c) Lots and lots of data
d) DATA written in capital letters

PSYCHOLOGY

Being a soccer coach is just like being a teacher. Both coaches and teachers want their players, or students, to learn, develop, be happy, and perform as well as they can. They also want them to be quiet when they're talking, not make too much of a mess, and not make faces behind their backs!

You know that teachers can be very different. Some are very strict; some love bad jokes. Some explain everything, and some leave you to figure things out.

And students are very different too. Some students do their homework as soon as possible, while others leave it until the last minute. Some pupils hate to speak in class, while others love the sound of their own voices.

The same is true in soccer. There are many coaching styles, and each player is different. The challenge for a coach is to find a style of leadership that gets the best out of each individual player and gets the whole team to improve. In order to do that, the coach needs to understand what makes each player respond: will the threat of punishment or an arm around the shoulder work best?

Coaches aren't just the people in charge of tactics. They are also **psychologists**, which is what we call people who are experts in how the human mind works.

Now, are you still listening at the back?

WHAT TYPE OF COACH ARE YA?

There are lots of different ways to lead a team. Look at these four famous coaches and see if any remind you of your favorite—or your least favorite—teacher!

1. THE HUGGER: JÜRGEN KLOPP

Teams coached: *Mainz 05, Borussia Dortmund, Liverpool*
The mood at the Liverpool Christmas party in 2016 was low. Earlier in the day, the team had lost to Watford. But coach Jürgen Klopp did not want the players to be sad. He told everyone to forget about the game, have fun, and do a lot of dancing. He jumped onto the dance floor and made everyone laugh. This is one of the ways that Klopp gets the best out of his teams. His use of humor makes people like him—and if you like someone, you are likely to work hard for them!

Klopp spends 70 percent of his time keeping everyone happy. He believes that TEAM stands for: Together Everyone Achieves More. Klopp is often laughing on the touchline. He also hugs his players a lot to show that he cares about them. Scientific studies have shown that teammates who hug or touch each other a lot are more likely to be successful. Even if his team loses, Klopp's players still get a hug. "The emotion makes the difference," he says. Kloppo cares!

OTHER HUGGERS:
Emma Hayes
Antonio Conte
Jorge Jesus
Diego Simeone

2. THE DEEP THINKER: PEP GUARDIOLA

Teams coached: Barcelona, Bayern Munich, Manchester City
All coaches want to beat their opponents. Pep Guardiola spends hours watching videos to work out weaknesses in other teams. Friends say he can only switch off for thirty-two minutes before he starts thinking about soccer again!

Guardiola is not afraid to come up with new solutions to win games. He famously switched Lionel Messi's position at Barcelona to help make him one of the world's best players. On the same team, Zlatan Ibrahimović was sold because he did not fit in with Pep's ideas. Guardiola regularly puts fullbacks in midfield or even midfielders on defense if he feels it will help the team use the ball better.

OTHER THINKERS:
Marcelo Bielsa
Mauricio Pochettino
Jorge Sampaoli
Thomas Tuchel

His players call him a perfectionist. He believes that soccer should be played in a certain way: by keeping possession of the ball for as long as possible before creating chances. If the players are willing to learn, he is a teacher who will challenge them to the limit and lead them to great victories.

3. THE QUIET LEADER: CARLO ANCELOTTI

Teams coached: *Reggiana, Parma, Juventus, AC Milan, Chelsea, Paris Saint-Germain, Real Madrid, Bayern Munich*

Carlo Ancelotti is known for being naturally quiet and open-minded. He will often change his ideas to find the right solution. He's coached some of the best teams in the world and is liked wherever he goes. That's impressive!

It helps that Ancelotti speaks lots of languages. He was also a successful player, winning three Italian league titles and two European Cups. He played in midfield, where he was known for quietly making things happen.

He is similar as a coach: he can fit into any team environment and get results. The loudest person in the room is not always the best; Ancelotti speaks quietly and rarely, but when he does, it's worth listening. Often Ancelotti lets players decide on the strategy they want to use for games.

He does not have a preferred style of soccer. When he was coach at Juventus, he changed the team's system to accommodate the great French midfielder Zinedine Zidane. At Real Madrid, he moved things around to get the best out of forward Cristiano Ronaldo. The skill of the quiet leader is to look like you are not doing too much, when actually you are.

OTHER QUIET LEADERS:
Didier Deschamps
Chris Hughton
Fernando Santos
Zinedine Zidane

4. THE TEACHER: ARSÈNE WENGER

Teams coached: Nancy, Monaco, Nagoya Grampus Eight, Arsenal

One newspaper ran the headline "Arsène Who?" when English team Arsenal appointed Arsène Wenger as coach in 1996. Everyone soon knew exactly who he was. The Frenchman quickly won three Premier League titles, including the 2003–2004 season, during which the team did not lose a single game. Invincible!

Wenger's success at Arsenal changed many things in soccer. Teams followed his approach to nutrition: he banned candy, chocolate, and soda from the training ground. He also introduced regular stretching sessions for his players before practice. Some of his older players said this allowed them to play for an extra few years. Other teams became less nervous about appointing foreign coaches and signing foreign players.

Wenger's key principle was to pick young players and help them improve. He was not afraid to select even very young players. "He is a teacher first, a manager second, a tactician third," said one Arsenal fan who knows him. Wenger said of his own influence: "I felt like I was opening the door to the rest of the world."

OTHER TEACHERS:
Jill Ellis
Eddie Howe
Leonardo Jardim
Óscar Tabárez

THE NAME'S BONDING . . .
TEAM BONDING

A good coach is always looking for ways to help the team bond. After all, if you understand and like your teammates, you may try that bit harder to help them on the field. Here are some wacky methods that coaches have tried:

SHEEP-HERDING

When he was Burnley coach, Eddie Howe wanted his players to raise the *baa* (get it?), so he took them on a surprise trip to a farm in Bristol. They were split into two groups, and each group had to round up ten sheep and herd them into a pen in the middle of a field. At the time, he thought it was a good exercise in leadership and teamwork. He later admitted that he got annoyed with some of the players. "It was a moment, for me, of understanding that with the modern player there are some things you can't do," Howe said. "Sheep-herding might be one of them."

SWAN LAKE

Graham Potter has been the most successful coach in the history of Östersunds FK, a small team based in Sweden. Since Potter joined the team in 2011, ÖFK has gone from the fourth division to the first division—thanks to some unique managerial methods. Every year, Potter asks his players to work together on a cultural project. One year they collaborated to write a book. In 2016,

they performed a modern dance version of the 1877 ballet *Swan Lake*. "If you want to develop them as people, you have to have those uncomfortable experiences," Potter said. "As a team, if we all understand that, then we can help each other."

PIZZA FLIPPING

To reward his Leicester City players for not conceding a goal in a game against Crystal Palace, Coach Claudio Ranieri took them out for a pizza-making lesson. The whole squad joined in, flipping dough and adding their own toppings. "It's the team spirit, and they enjoy training," said Italian boss Ranieri. "A little bit of luck is important. Luck is the salt, the fans are the tomato—with no tomato there is no pizza." It did the trick: Leicester went on to win the Premier League. *Bravissimo*, Claudio!

BINGO!

Leeds United was English champion twice under coach Don Revie, back in 1969 and 1974. The former Leeds player immediately fostered a united spirit in the squad. He organized social nights for the players and their families, which included playing dominoes and bingo. "Our whole ethos was built on loyalty," said midfielder Peter Lorimer. "We all fight for each other; we all work for each other." That's true teamwork.

THE CLOCK IS TICKING

Being a soccer coach is a powerful job—but it could be over very quickly. You are responsible for the team results, which might affect the size of the TV broadcast and team sponsorship deals. You also need to keep everyone fully motivated and ready to give their all—not just the eleven players who start each game, but the others who are not picked. It's important that the fans and owners like you too. Here are some coach appointments that didn't work out so well:

Coach: Leroy Rosenior
How long in the job: 10 minutes
Team/Year: Torquay, 2007
Reason: Just after he was hired, a new owner came in and fired him.

Coach: Marcelo Bielsa
How long in the job: 2 days
Team/Year: Lazio, 2016
Reason: The players he was promised would be bought were not, and so he left.

Coach: Dave Bassett
How long in the job: 4 days
Team/Year: Crystal Palace, 1984
Reason: Bassett realized he preferred his old team, Wimbledon, so he went back.

FERGIE'S LIFE LESSONS

Sir Alex Ferguson was Manchester United's most successful coach ever. He once discussed his best coaching tips, which we list here. At Soccer School, we think these are great ideas to follow.

1. Start with the foundation.
2. Dare to rebuild.
3. Set high standards.
4. Never give up control.
5. Match the message to the moment.
6. Prepare to win.
7. Rely on the power of observation.
8. Never stop adapting.

HUGGY SLAPPS

☆ STAR STUDENT

FREE ♥ HUGS

66 I'm in charge! 99

☆☆☆ STAR STUDENT **Stats**

Longest time spent not thinking about soccer: 8 mins.
Management books read: 26
Life lessons in notebook: 137
High: 5!
Birthplace: Boss, Missouri
Supports: Kaizer Chiefs (South Africa)
Fave player: Grant Leadbitter
Trick: Brings the team together

PSYCHOLOGY QUIZ

1. What is a psychologist?

a) Someone who is an expert in the human mind and human behavior

b) Someone who can tell the future

c) Someone who can score three goals in every game

d) An expert in dancing to the PSY song "Gangnam Style"

2. What is a perfectionist?

a) Someone who is perfect

b) Someone who loves perfect people

c) Someone who only accepts perfection

d) Someone who purrs

3. How many people took part in the largest group hug in the world, recorded in Canada in 2010?

a) 1,055

b) 10,554

c) 105,554

d) 1,554,000

4. Which of the following coaches is a hugger?

a) Zinedine Zidane

b) Antonio Conte

c) Eddie Howe

d) Thomas Tuchel

5. Why did Arsène Wenger ban sodas from the training ground?

a) The players kept burping during games.

b) Too much sugar was bad for the players.

c) The floor was always sticky because they spilled the drinks.

d) The players were peeing too much.

HEALTH
AFTER-SCHOOL
CLUB

SMOOTHIE BAR

What soccer players eat and drink is important not only on game day but all season long. Players try to eat the healthiest foods to keep their fitness up and performance levels high. In this after-school club, we'll show you how easy it is to make a healthy snack at home. Just throwing some fruit and vegetables into a blender can have amazing results! Here are some easy smoothie recipes that everyone at Soccer School loves. Fruity fun!

Put a Lid on it!

Smoothie 1:
Ben's Banana Bonanza

Bananas are packed with nutrients that are great for your body: potassium, which is good for your heart, carbohydrates to give you energy, and fiber to improve your digestion. The nuts contain protein, which builds cells and muscles in your body.

Ingredients: *1 banana, a handful of walnuts, 2 cups milk, 1 tbsp honey*
Could also add: *Peanut butter, pineapple, cocoa powder, blueberries, ginger*

GOOD FOR: Boosting energy before training
TASTE SENSATION: 1/3

Smoothie 2: Spike's C-Blaster

This refreshing smoothie made from fruits high in vitamin C will protect your body in winter and help you recover after practice. Vitamin C boosts our immune system and helps us fight off colds and other illnesses. You don't want to have the sniffles when you're taking a shot with just the goalie to beat!

Ingredients: 1 grapefruit (peeled), 1 cup pineapple chunks, 1 cup strawberries, ½ cup yogurt
Could also add: mango, orange, kiwi, raspberries, kale

GOOD FOR: Recovery after practice and fighting off illness
TASTE SENSATION: 2/3

Smoothie 3: Alex's 'Ave-A-Go Avocado

Some scientists claim that certain fruits, such as blueberries and avocados, are really good for the brain. They're certainly delicious, whatever effect they have. Alex loves both blueberries and avocados, so maybe that's why he's good at math!

Ingredients: ½ avocado (peeled), 1 cup blueberries, 1 cup yogurt, ½ cup milk, juice from ½ lime
Could also add: blackberries, apple, beet, lemon

GOOD FOR: Overall well-being
TASTE SENSATION: 3/3

FOOD NOTE! Always ask an adult to help you chop the fruit and use a blender. If you are diabetic or have food allergies, ask an adult first.

ART

E very soccer team has a symbol.
This symbol—called a badge, crest, or logo—appears on the team's shirts. It has a practical use: to identify members of that team. But it has another use too. The shapes, colors, and words on the badge reflect the team's history and its values. It's as if everything about the team is captured in the badge, which is one reason why many players like to kiss it when they score a goal.

The Soccer School badge has two 18-yard boxes, a soccer ball, a book, and a gold star. These are things that we think say a lot about Soccer School—that it's a place for fun, for soccer, for learning, and for stars!

Many team badges are inspired by **coats of arms**, which were symbols historically used by armies, rich families, towns, and businesses. In this lesson, you are going to learn how to create a coat of arms. This coat of arms will tell the story of who you are. And if you ever have your own soccer team, it can be your team badge too.

Let's get our coats!

A STITCH IN TIME

Before we start designing our coat of arms, let's take a closer look at what they are and where they came from.

In 1066, the English army was defeated at the Battle of Hastings by an invading force of Normans led by William the Conqueror. Back then there were no cameras. So to remember the victory, a piece of cloth, 75 yards/69 meters long, was embroidered to show different scenes from the battle, such as the moment the English king Harold was supposedly killed by an arrow to the eye. Eek! This giant piece of cloth is now known as the Bayeux Tapestry.

The tapestry gives us a rare glimpse of what soldiers wore in those days and what equipment they used. And it shows us that some of the soldiers used shields decorated with specific, recognizable images. For example, some shields bore a cross, and some an animal. Historians think the armies put these symbols on the shields so the soldiers could quickly see who was a friend and who was an enemy—quite a useful thing to be sure of when you are in the middle of fighting! There was no point writing words on the shields since few soldiers could read.

These military symbols later became known as coats of arms because they were displayed on tunics worn over armor. The system of rules for the design and use of coats of arms is called **heraldry**.

HARK THE HERALDRY

A couple of hundred years after the Battle of Hastings, rich and powerful individuals began to copy soldiers, using coats of arms as symbols for their own families. And later, towns and counties got in on the act too, using coats of arms as their symbols.

Then it was soccer's turn to get involved. In 1875, Blackburn Rovers were the first team in England to wear a symbol on their uniform. The team had a Maltese cross, seen on the flag on the left, on the left breast of their shirts. The cross is a symbol associated with knights, and each of its eight points symbolizes a specific character trait: truth, faith, repentance, humility, justice, mercy, sincerity, and bravery. That was a lot for the Rovers players to think about!

Other teams adopted their local council's coat of arms. In 1877, Notts County, for example, started wearing a badge with three crowns and a ragged cross on their uniforms—the City of Nottingham's crest. This may have been because Notts County's lineup was made up of Nottingham's upper class, many of whom played on school rugby teams that sported similar symbols on their shirts.

He was great at dealing with crosses!

CLASH OF SYMBOLS

OBJECT	SYMBOLIC MEANING
Apple	Happiness
Bay Leaf	Poet
Grapes	Truth
Hand	Faith
Olive branch	Peace
Seashell	Traveler
Sword	Justice

A coat of arms has several distinctive parts. It normally has a **shield**, two animals that support the shield, known as **shield supporters**, and a short piece of text called a **motto**. The shield can be any shape or color you like and may be decorated with different objects. The animals can also be anything you like—even mythological creatures.

Traditionally, however, the objects, colors, and creatures on a coat of arms were understood to be symbols that

COLOR	SYMBOLIC MEANING
Blue	Loyalty
Gold	Generosity
Green	Hope
Orange	Ambition
Purple	Royalty
White	Peace

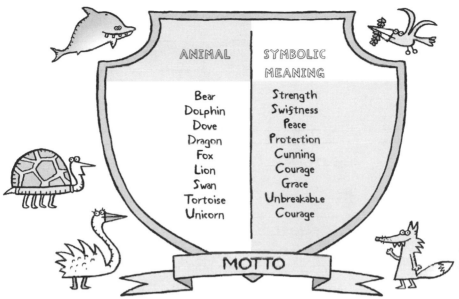

ANIMAL	SYMBOLIC MEANING
Bear	Strength
Dolphin	Swiftness
Dove	Peace
Dragon	Protection
Fox	Cunning
Lion	Courage
Swan	Grace
Tortoise	Unbreakable
Unicorn	Courage

MOTTO

represented something else. For example, an apple meant happiness, a lion meant courage, and blue meant loyalty. Using symbols on your coat of arms was a way to show people the skills and attributes you valued and the kind of person you were.

On these pages are some of the meanings of things found on coats of arms. Below are some objects and symbols we invented for modern times:

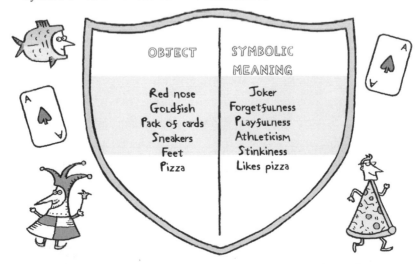

OBJECT	SYMBOLIC MEANING
Red nose	Joker
Goldfish	Forgetfulness
Pack of cards	Playfulness
Sneakers	Athleticism
Feet	Stinkiness
Pizza	Likes pizza

WHAT A MOTTO LOTTO!

Another important part of a coat of arms is the motto. A motto is a short phrase that sums up your beliefs or way of approaching life. Here are Alex's and Ben's:

> **ALEX:**
> **FAMILIA + NUMERI X ROTAE**
> **= GAUDIUM**
> (Family + math X wheels = happiness)
>
> **BEN: FAMILIA, RISUS ET PIZZA**
> (Family together, with laughter and pizza)

Mottoes can be in any language you like, but many people choose Latin, the language of ancient Rome that no one speaks anymore. Professor Mary Beard of the University of Cambridge says that Latin is perfect for mottoes because it can make things sound snappier and shorter and cleverer than they would in English. Professor Beard says her department is always getting requests from charities and sports teams to translate English phrases into Latin.

Some soccer teams still have Latin mottoes on their badges. Bury has *Vincit Omnia Industria*, which is Latin for "Hard Work Conquers All," while Blackburn Rovers has *Arte et Labore*, Latin for "By Skill and Hard Work." (There are a few different ways of saying *hard work* in Latin!) Other teams, listed on the next page, used to have Latin mottoes on their badges but have removed them in recent years:

CAVE CANEM*

*BEWARE OF THE DOG

TEAM	LATIN MOTTO	TRANSLATION
Arsenal	Victoria Concordia Crescit	Victory through Harmony
Manchester City	Superbia in Proelio	Pride in Battle
Tottenham Hotspur	Audere est Facere	To Dare Is to Do

MARVELOUS MOTTOES

Here are some of our favorite team mottoes:

Team: Asante Kotoko (Ghana)
Motto: *Kum Apem A, Apem Beba* (Asante Twi)
Meaning: Kill a thousand, and a thousand more will come

Team: Queen's Park (Scotland)
Motto: *Ludere Causa Ludendi* (Latin)
Meaning: To play for the sake of playing

Team: Barcelona (Spain)
Motto: *Més que un club* (Catalan)
Meaning: More than a club

Team: Liverpool (England)
Motto: You'll Never Walk Alone

Team: Sporting Lisbon (Portugal)
Motto: *Esforço, Dedicação, Devoção, Glória* (Portuguese)
Meaning: Effort, dedication, devotion, glory

BIG ARMS

Here are our versions of some really cool soccer badges from around the world to give you inspiration for making yours.

Sampdoria (Italy): Sampdoria's shield includes an image of an old sailor called Baciccia, known as *lupo di mare* (wolf of the sea), with a pipe in his mouth. That's because Sampdoria is based in Genoa, Italy's biggest port city.

Bohemians (Czech Republic): Bohemians have a green kangaroo on their badge because they toured Australia in 1927 and were given two kangaroos to take home. We don't think they were green, though!

Ajax (the Netherlands): Ajax's badge features a drawing of the ancient Greek hero Ajax, who was known for his skills as a warrior. He is drawn with eleven separate lines to represent the eleven players in the team.

Valencia (Spain): The Spanish city has a bat on its coat of arms, and the soccer team has incorporated the same animal into its badge design. The bat opens its wings to wrap itself around the edge of the whole shield.

Gent (Belgium): Gent players call themselves the Buffalos, because in 1895 the American Buffalo Bill visited Belgium with his circus. The audience chanted, "Buffalo, buffalo!" during the show, and the words stuck. Soon fans were chanting them at Gent's games, which is how the team got its name.

And don't forget our coats of arms too:

ALEX

BEN

TERMS AND CONDITIONS APPLY

If you love your coat of arms, you might want to get it officially approved. The College of Arms, the official body that acts on powers given to it by the queen of England, charges around $10,000 to grant you your own personal coat of arms. The college told us that no professional soccer teams have ever been granted coats of arms. "Technically, their use of Arms is unlawful," they said. Naughty!

OTTO MOTTO

STAR STUDENT

Soccer School

66 On my chest! 99

STAR STUDENT **Stats**

Annis Latine: XII
Number of coats: 8
Number of arms: 2
Otto Motto's Lotto Numbers:
46, 12, 18, 23, 31, 6
Birthplace: South Shields, England
Supports: Arminia Bielefeld (Germany)
Fave player: Sebastián Coates
Trick: Silky Latin skills

ART QUIZ

1. Who do you need to ask for official permission to use a coat of arms?

a) The Arms Academy
b) The College of Arms
c) Arms R Us
d) Army McArmface

2. What does the Latin phrase *Magnus frater spectat te* mean?

a) Magnus farted while putting on his spectacles.
b) Big Brother is watching you.
c) You need to watch Magnus's brother.
d) Magnus's brother is watching you.

3. What mythical creature is on the Liverpool team badge?

a) Liverbird
b) Dragon
c) Unicorn
d) Yeti

4. Which Argentine team, where Lionel Messi began his career, has a black-and-red badge with the letters N.O.B. on it?

a) Nueva Olimpico Barracuda
b) Never Organize Birthdays
c) Neuquen Olimpo Brown
d) Newell's Old Boys

5. What is the image on the badge of Italian team Roma?

a) Gladiator Cassius Maximus fighting in the Colosseum
b) A she-wolf breastfeeding twins Romulus and Remus
c) A flight of doves
d) A soldier marching in a military parade

BUSINESS STUDIES

arning money is difficult, but sometimes spending it is the hardest part.

It's like when Ben wants a new pair of sneakers. He has the money in his pocket, but can't decide which pair to buy. His mind is full of questions:

Cheap vs. expensive?

Brightly colored vs. plain?

Light-up soles vs. self-lacing?

Laces vs. Velcro?

Ben must decide what he thinks is most important about his new pair of sneakers, and weigh this against the prices of the sneakers in the store. He must decide whether the shoes he wants are worth the money. This takes him forever!

The same process takes place whenever we go shopping, whether it's for sneakers, candy, toys, or cars. We ask ourselves: "Is this purchase worth the money?"

Today we'll talk about buying and selling soccer players. We'll see how teams decide whom to buy and, once they decide, how they go about it.

Deal?

THE PRICE IS RIGHT

When you buy a gallon of milk, you know what you're getting: a gallon of milk. You know that milk from one store is the same as milk from another store. You know that you need to drink it within a few days or it will go bad. And you know that all gallons of milk cost roughly the same.

Soccer players are not like milk. All soccer players are different, and they are worth very different amounts of money. Here are some factors that determine the price of a player:

International status: If someone plays for their country, they have a big showcase for their talent and will probably cost more. If a player has been picked for the national team, it shows that they are one of the very best in their country, which tends to make them more expensive.

Age: Players in their midtwenties are more expensive, because that's when most are playing at their best. Plus they can play for a team longer and have more resale value.

International status

Position: Strikers are often more expensive because they score the goals that make the difference between winning and losing. There is less separation of value with goalkeepers as so many are "Steady Eddies," which is why they tend to be the cheapest players.

Celebrity status: Sometimes teams are not just thinking about performance, but also how famous the player is. A star player with charisma will increase interest in the team, which means that the team can earn more money on merchandising and sponsorship. Companies pay lots of money to be associated with celebrities. As a result, celebrity players often sell for higher amounts of money.

Nationality: In the U.K., eight players out of twenty-five need to have come through an English soccer academy or training program, so there's a lot of competition to get the best English players. Since Major League Soccer in North America is still growing in size and popularity, American and Canadian teams are likely to pay more for talented foreign players (who count as domestic players if they have a green card) in order to improve the quality of play and increase the number of fans.

COMPLICATED CONTRACTS

Another reason soccer players are different from milk is that it is straightforward to buy a gallon of milk. You pay the money and you get the milk, which belongs to you forever (until you pee it out).

When a team buys a player, the process is much more complicated. For one thing, a team cannot buy a player forever. You buy them for a fixed amount of time, which will be stated in the **contract**, which is a document that sets out all the terms and conditions of the purchase. Both the player and the team must **sign** the contract, which is why we use the word *sign* when talking about players joining teams. When a player joins a team, we can say that they signed with that team or that the team has signed the player.

When a team signs a top player, they will try to sign that player for a long period of time to prevent a rival team from trying to sign them. Players nearing the end of their contracts are often much cheaper than players at the beginning or in the middle of their contracts, because at the end of the contract, the selling team will no longer own the player and will therefore get nothing at all from a transfer.

RISKY BUSINESS

Soccer players are a high-risk purchase. You never know how a player will adapt to their new team. Players fail to adapt because they:

- ⚽ Miss their family
- ⚽ Receive different tactical demands
- ⚽ Can't speak the language
- ⚽ Don't like living in a new home
- ⚽ Feel the weather is too cold/hot
- ⚽ Get injured
- ⚽ Are too busy partying

Sometimes the risk of buying an expensive player pays off. Real Madrid spent $131.5 million on Cristiano Ronaldo—a HUGE amount of money, but you never hear the fans complaining about his contribution to the team. He has helped them win two league titles and three Champions League titles, as well as smashing the all-time scoring record with over four hundred goals for the team. And he's won four Ballon d'Or titles for the world's best player. He's a bargain! Plus his name sells an enormous amount of merchandise for his team.

MOST EXPENSIVE PLAYERS IN THE WORLD

PLAYER	DATE	FROM	TO	AMOUNT ($)
Gareth Bale	2013	Tottenham Hotspur	Real Madrid	$132 million
Cristiano Ronaldo	2009	Manchester United	Real Madrid	$131.5 million
Paul Pogba	2016	Juventus	Manchester United	$116.4 million
Gonzalo Higuain	2016	Napoli	Juventus	$99 million
Luis Suárez	2014	Liverpool	Barcelona	$85.5 million

HOW TO MAKE TRANSFERS STICK

A player moving from one team to another — usually when one is buying and the other is selling — is called a **transfer**. The process has several stages:

1. SCOUTING

A team looking for a new player comes up with a list of names. They factor in position, age, speed, height, ability, budget, and potential to improve. The team has a short list of up to ten names and starts by trying to buy their first choice.

2. INQUIRY

If a team is interested in a player who is under contract elsewhere, they need written permission from the player's current team to talk to him. Most professional players have an **agent**, who is the person who handles their business affairs. Usually, the interested team gets in touch with the agent of their first-choice player and then makes an official approach if the player is open to a move.

3. NEGOTIATIONS

Senior officials at the two teams will negotiate a price, via e-mail, text message, phone, or in person. Transfers can break down at this stage, because teams have different valuations of players. The payment structure also has to be discussed: teams might pay the whole sum up front, but most pay in **installments** over several periods, sometimes lasting years.

4. PERSONAL TERMS AND CLAUSES

The deal is not done until a contract is written up between the player and the new team. The contract includes details of how long the player will be with the team, monthly salary, and any bonuses that may be due for games played, goals scored, or trophies won. The buying team may also put in a **clause**—the word used by lawyers for a detail in the contract—that states that if the team is demoted to a lower league, they can reduce the salary.

5. MEDICAL

Before the deal is completed, the buying team will give the player a thorough medical exam to make sure there are no underlying injuries. It includes a comprehensive heart screening and a check on the lower back and pelvic joints, which impact mobility. Goalkeepers have extra tests on their shoulders, elbows, and wrists. Some teams even include vision and hearing tests.

ALEX, I said SOME TEAMS EVEN INCLUDE VISION AND HEARING TESTS!

6. FINAL TOUCH

The transfer is complete once the details are registered with the league.

ONE EXTRA SCOOP, PLEASE!

Sometimes it's not money that changes hands for a transfer.

A FREEZER FULL OF ICE CREAM

Hugh McLenahan, Stockport to Manchester United (1927)

English selling team Stockport was holding a fund-raising event to ease its financial troubles, and so United's assistant coach, Louis Rocca, whose family ran an ice-cream business, sent two freezers full of ice cream in return for the defender. McLenahan played over one hundred games and was even the United captain for a while. Chilly business!

BODY WEIGHT IN SHRIMP

Kenneth Kristensen, Vindbjart to Fløy (2002)

What a great catch! Third-division Norwegian team Fløy wanted to sign a striker from rivals Vindbjart, who decided that asking for the player's body weight in shrimp would be a good deal. They played each other the following weekend: Kristensen weighed in at 165 pounds/ 75 kilograms, and the deal was done. Shrimple!

30 SWEAT SUITS

Zat Knight, Rushall Olympic to Fulham (1999)

Fulham made quite a profit on Knight, whom they bought from nonleague team Rushall Olympic. They did not have to pay anything, but owner Mohamed Al-Fayed sent thirty sweat suits by way of thanks. Knight ended up playing for England and was sold to Aston Villa for $7.2 million. Hope the sweats were nice!

CLAUSE CONFUSION

Some contracts have very strange clauses:

Player: Spencer Prior
Team: Cardiff City
Clause: The player had to eat sheep's testicles after joining. Team owner Sam Hammam

was a fun-loving businessman from Lebanon, where the food is a delicacy when served with a lemon-and-parsley sauce. Hammam added the clause for a laugh. Baaaaa-d!

Player: Mario Balotelli
Team: Liverpool
Clause: The Italian forward came with a reputation for misbehaving on the field, so was told that he would get a reward if he was sent off FEWER than four times in one season and did NOT spit on an opponent. He shouldn't be doing that anyway! He managed to behave. His reward? $1.5 million!

Player: Dennis Bergkamp
Team: Arsenal
Clause: Bergkamp insisted on a clause stating that he never needed to travel to away games by plane, since he was scared of flying.

Player: Stefan Schwarz

Team: Sunderland

Clause: Not allowed to fly into space. His agent had signed up for a flight on one of the first passenger flights into space, and the buying team was worried that he would take the Swedish midfielder with him. It never happened. And Schwarz got the nickname "Spaceman."

SELMA STRYKER

STAR ☆STUDENT

66 Let's make a deal! 99

☆☆ STAR ☆STUDENT Stats

Number of clauses in contract: 26

Number of subclauses in contract: 431

Number of Santa Clauses: 1

Birthplace: Newmarket, England

Supports: Fortuna Düsseldorf (Germany)

Fave player: Diego Costa

Trick: Fastest at signing autographs

BUSINESS STUDIES QUIZ

1. Which player position usually goes for the least money in the transfer market?

a) Goalkeeper
b) Defender
c) Midfielder
d) Striker

2. According to his contract, what was Norwegian defender Stig Inge Bjørnebye forbidden from doing while a Liverpool player in the 1990s?

a) Ski jumping
b) Fishing for trout
c) Painting
d) Scoring

3. What does ITC stand for?

a) Intense Transfer Confusion
b) Insane Transfer Contract
c) Immediate Transfer Clause
d) International Transfer Certificate

4. Which player was Crystal Palace striker Christian Benteke especially pleased that his team signed in summer 2016?

a) His uncle Steve Mandanda
b) His best friend Mathieu Flamini
c) His brother Jonathan Benteke
d) His hero Andros Townsend

5. What was left-back Cohen Bramall's job before Arsenal signed him from seventh-division team Hednesford Town in January 2017?

a) Car factory worker
b) Fortune cookie writer
c) Gym personal trainer
d) Dog-surfing instructor

SNOOZE FEST

It's the end of the week, so time to reward yourself with some decent relaxation. Soccer players need sleep and recovery time to perform at their best: they must sleep for the right amount of time and make sure they relax in the right way between games. This after-school club is all about how to relax—but you need to be switched on to know how to switch off!

Ben "The Pen" is Zen

Relax 1: Keep it dark and cool

Ninety minutes before the time you want to fall asleep, switch off all electronic devices—phones, tablets, laptops. That's the same time as a soccer game! Make sure your bedroom is as dark as possible, and keep it at a cool temperature.

GOOD FOR: Achieving peak performance the next day
RECOVERY RATING: 1/4

Relax 2: Muscle love

You need to be lying in bed for this one. Take a deep breath, tense your toes and feet for a few seconds, and then breathe out slowly. Tighten your lower leg muscles for a few secs, release, then continue up the body: flex your upper legs, tummy area, lower back, chest and upper back, hands, and arms.

GOOD FOR: Relieving tension in muscles
RECOVERY RATING: 2/4

ReLax 3: Picture this

Think of something you really, really want. Maybe it is getting onto the school soccer team, getting a good grade on some homework, or even baking a cake. Then think about all the steps you need to go through in order to achieve your goal. For each step, focus on the images in your mind. Sometimes imagining the step-by-step process of what you need to do—a technique called visualizing—can actually help that thing happen!

GOOD FOR: Reducing anxiety, focusing on steps needed to reach goals
RECOVERY RATING: 3/4

ReLax 4: 4-7-8 trick

This is a yoga exercise that experts think can make you fall asleep within one minute! Put the tip of your tongue just behind your upper front teeth and keep it there. Then take a big breath and let it out through your mouth around your tongue. Close your mouth and breathe in quietly through your nose for four seconds. Hold your breath for seven seconds. Exhale through your mouth for eight seconds. Repeat three times. This exercise can take two months to perfect, but then you'll be counting the z's in no time!

GOOD FOR: Relaxing the body and staying calm
RECOVERY RATING: 4/4

QUIZ ANSWERS

HEALTH (11)
1. d
2. b
3. a
4. a
5. b

FOREIGN LANGUAGES (29)
1. b
2. c
3. c
4. a
5. c

PHYSICS (41)
1. d
2. c
3. c
4. a
5. c

HISTORY (55)
1. b
2. d
3. a
4. a
5. d

BOTANY (67)
1. b
2. d
3. d
4. a
5. b

FILM STUDIES (81)
1. b
2. a
3. b
4. d
5. b

ENGINEERING (99)
1. d
2. d
3. b
4. c
5. c

ENGLISH (111)
1. a
2. c
3. b
4. a
5. c

RELIGIOUS STUDIES (125)
1. a
2. a (Gabriel Jesus and Jesus Navas)
3. b
4. d
5. c

BIOLOGY (141)
1. d
2. b
3. c
4. b
5. b

MATH (153)
1. b
2. d
3. a
4. b
5. c

PSYCHOLOGY (165)
1. a
2. c
3. b
4. b
5. b

ART (179)
1. b
2. b
3. a
4. d
5. b

BUSINESS STUDIES (191)
1. a
2. a
3. d
4. c
5. a

ACKNOWLEDGMENTS

The winner of Soccer School's Man of the Game award goes to illustrator Spike Gerrell. He always scores when he draws!

The team at Walker Books is brilliantly talented in strength and depth. We are grateful to captain Daisy "DJ" Jellicoe and her teammates Denise Johnstone-Burt, Louise Jackson, Laurelie Bazin, Jenny Bish, Simon Armstrong, Alex Spears, Rosi Crawley, and Kirsten Cozens.

Thanks again to our top-notch backroom staff at Janklow & Nesbit, Rebecca Carter, Rebecca Folland, and Kirsty Gordon; and at David Luxton Associates, David Luxton, Rebecca Winfield, and Nick Walters.

We would like to thank the following experts for sharing their knowledge with us: Roma Agrawal, Duncan Alexander, Marcus Alves, Dr. Anthony Bale, Jack Bates, Dr. Lucja Biel, Charlie Brooks, Mads Burheim, Dr. David Carey, Dr. Mick Chappell, Peter Chipcase, Rhys Courtney, Avi Creditor, Michiel de Hoog, Wink de Putter, Taras Dolinsky, Dave Farrar, Caroline Federman, Daniel Geey, Manleen Gill, Gemma Gordon, Matt Grace, Jonathan Harding, Martyn Heather, Alex Holiga, Raphael Honigstein, Gary Hughes, Dr. Paul Ibbotson, Motoko Jitsukawa, Uğur Karakullukçu, Sergio Krithinas, Christopher Lash, John Ledwidge, Ronnie Leyman, Ian Lynam, Karen Maxwell, Prof. Chris McManus, Steve McNally, Ben Miller, Mike Murphy at Steaditec, Venkat Nallamilli, Ben Oakley, Peter O'Donoghue, Rafael Ortega, Amanda Overend, Lauren Pearson, Tim Reeves, Emre Sarigul, Ionica Smeets, Harry Stopes, Prof. Stefan Szymanski, Benjamin Thompsett, David Winner, Nia Wyn Thomas, and Michal Zachodny. Special thanks to Opta for all the data in the Math lesson.

Cheers to our Star Students: Oscar Auerbach, Thomas Elks, Harry McAllester, Flora Pretor-Pinney, Ronnie Thomas-Armstrong, and Cass Yechiel.

Ben would like to thank Annie for her inspiration and support, and Clemmy and Bibi for making him laugh every day and making sure the jokes in this book are up to scratch.

Alex would like to thank Nat for being his family's star player, and Zak and Barnaby for the team hugs.

ABOUT YOUR COACHES

Alex Bellos writes for the *Guardian*. He has written several best-selling popular science books and created two mathematical coloring books. He loves puzzles.

Ben Lyttleton is a journalist, broadcaster, and soccer consultant. He has written books about how to score the perfect penalty and what we can learn from soccer's best coaches.

Spike Gerrell grew up loving both playing soccer and drawing pictures. He now gets to draw for a living. At heart, though, he will always be a central midfielder.

MORE FROM SOCCER SCHOOL

Look for the next book in the series:
Soccer School Season 3!

Find out more at
www.soccerschoolseries.com.
Find Soccer School
on YouTube too!